Russian Airlines

Airlines
and their Aircraft

Dmitriy Komissarov and Yefim Gordon

MIDLAND
An imprint of
Ian Allan Publishing

Russian Airlines and their Aircraft
© 2004 Dmitriy Komissarov and Yefim Gordon

ISBN 1 85780 176 8

Published by Midland Publishing
4 Watling Drive, Hinckley, LE10 3EY, England
Tel: 01455 254 490   Fax: 01455 254 495
E-mail: midlandbooks@compuserve.com

Midland Publishing is an imprint of
Ian Allan Publishing Ltd

Worldwide distribution (except North America):
Midland Counties Publications
4 Watling Drive, Hinckley, LE10 3EY, England
Telephone: 01455 254 450   Fax: 01455 233 737
E-mail: midlandbooks@compuserve.com
www.midlandcountiessuperstore.com

North American trade distribution:
Specialty Press Publishers & Wholesalers Inc.
39966 Grand Avenue, North Branch, MN 55056, USA
Tel: 651 277 1400   Fax: 651 277 1203
Toll free telephone: 800 895 4585
www.specialtypress.com

Design concept and layout
© 2004 Midland Publishing and
Polygon Press Ltd. (Moscow, Russia)
Line drawings by V. I. Klimov and Polygon-Press

This book is illustrated with photos by Dmitriy
Komissarov, Yefim Gordon, Yuriy Kirsanov, Yuriy
Kotel'nikov, Dmitriy Petrochenko and Il'dar Valeyev,
as well as from the archive of the Russian Aviation
Research Trust.

Printed in England by Ian Allan Printing Ltd
Riverdene Business Park, Molesey Road,
Hersham, Surrey, KT12 4RG

Contents

Acknowledgements

The authors wish to express their sincere thanks to
the people who assisted in making this book:

Yuriy Kotel'nikov, Viktor Kravchenko, Il'dar Valeyev,
Peter Davison, Mike Kell and especially Dmitriy
Petrochenko and Yuriy Kirsanov, who supplied many
of the high-quality photos used in this book; Nikolay
Nalobin and Stanislav Looshchik of Vnukovo Airport
Aviation Security and Aleksandr Boonaryov of East
Line Aviation Security who granted ramp access,
allowing valuable photos to be taken, as well as the
security officers who accompanied the authors on
the ramp; Lidia Anghelova, Natal'ya Titova and Ivan
Faleyev at the CIS Interstate Aviation Committee; the
editorial team of Soviet Transports (Peter Hillman,
Stuart Jessup, Guus Ottenhof and Tony Morris), as
well as Nikolay Ionkin, for supplying hot information
on aircraft movements and construction numbers;
Nigel Eastaway of the Russian Aviation Research
Trust, whose extensive archive proved very useful;
and, last but not least, Tatiana Lyukhanova, Tatiana
Moorina, Sergey Chaboonin, Mikhail Kvashnin and
Andrey Samoylov at Polygon Press for their dedica-
tion, perseverance and a lot of overtime work.

The Russian airline scene became extremely varied in the early 1990s, and so it has remained ever since.
Here, Kirov Air Enterprise Tu-134A-3 RA-65060 (c/n (73)49872, f/n 4002) sits parked at Moscow/Vnukovo-1,
with a resident Vnukovo Airlines Tu-154M and an Aero Rent Tu-134AK in the background. *Mike Kell*

Russian Airlines: Past & Present

The former USSR was characterised by a 'single-party system' – no political parties were tolerated except the omnipotent Communist Party of the Soviet Union, and any deviations from the 'party line' were resolutely stomped out. Similarly, for most of the Soviet Union's history the nation's civil aviation scene was characterised by a 'single-airline system' – Aeroflot Soviet Airlines was a 'one size fits all' behemoth which catered for all civil air transportation needs, provided air services in the interests of the agricultural industry and various government agencies and so forth.

Originally (until the late 1950s) the Soviet Union's civil aviation system was structured according to the role division principle, consisting of a whole range of departments responsible for different kinds of aerial work. These included the Main Directorate of the Civil Air Fleet (GU GVF – *Glahvnoye oopravleniye grazhdahnskovo vozdooshnovo flota*) which operated scheduled passenger/cargo services, the Main Directorate of the Northern Sea Route (GU SMP – *Glahvnoye oopravleniye severnovo morskovo putee*) which included the Polar Aviation branch, an agricultural division, an air ambulance division, a geological prospecting division (the Aerogheologiya trust), a photo survey division etc.

Later the system was reorganised according to the territorial principle, the vast territory of the Soviet Union being divided between a number of Civil Aviation Directorates (UGA – *Oopravleniye grazhdahnskoy aviahtsii*), several of which were situated in the Russian Federation and one in each of the other constituent Soviet republics. Thus Aeroflot's organization closely resembled an air arm's order of battle – which is hardly surprising, considering that the Soviet civil air fleet constituted an immediately available military reserve. (The reader may be interested to know that civil aircraft registrations were issued by the General Headquarters of the Soviet Air Force, not by the Ministry of Civil Aviation.) The CADs were broadly equivalent to the air forces of the USAF or the air armies of the Soviet Air Force. Each CAD comprised a number of United Air Detachments (OAO – *obyedinyonnyy aviaotryad*) based in major cities – or airports, if a large city had several airports; these were equivalent to an air group (USAF) or an air division (SovAF). Each UAD consisted of several Flights (LO – *lyotnyy otryad*) similar to an air wing (USAF) or an air regiment (SovAF). Finally, a Flight comprised up to four, or maybe more, squadrons (*aviaeskadril'ya*); quite often different squadrons of the same Flight operated different aircraft types. Some Flights included Independent Air Squadrons (*otdel'naya aviaeskadril'ya*) which were based elsewhere.

Over the years the structure changed somewhat; for instance, the former Northern Territorial CAD was disbanded, the Arkhangel'sk, Komi and Leningrad CADs being formed instead, while the Siberian CAD was split into the East Siberian and West Siberian directorates. The Polar Aviation Directorate persisted until the early 1970s but was then dissolved, its functions (support of Soviet Arctic and Antarctic research stations etc.) passing to other directorates (notably the Krasnoyarsk CAD) which supplied aircraft as required.

When Mikhail S. Gorbachov launched his new policy of *perestroika* (restructuring) in 1985, an unprecedented liberalisation of the Soviet economy began, but it was another five years before anyone challenged the monopoly of Aeroflot. 1990 saw the appearance of two new Soviet airlines, Transaero and Volga-Dnepr. The subsequent dissolution of the Soviet Union in 1991 inevitably led to the disintegration of the 'all-Union' Aeroflot. (True, Aeroflot remained in existence as Russia's flag carrier, but that was a pale shadow of its former self – see below.) Some parts of Aeroflot (the former Estonian, Latvian and Lithuanian CADs) found themselves outside the newly-established Commonwealth of Independent States. In the CIS, the Civil Aviation Directorates were reorganised into

In Soviet times the nation's civil aviation needs were catered for by one huge airline, Aeroflot. Here, Tu-104B CCCP-42480 lands at Moscow-Vnukovo past IL-18s and an IL-14. *Yefim Gordon archive*

Regional Air Transport Directorates and the many United Air Detachments became new airlines as the former Soviet republics steered towards the free market. In the Russian Federation alone, as many as 400 airlines big and small (in fact, some operated only a single aircraft) were registered in the early 1990s.

The 'deregulation' of Aeroflot was a painful process. The newcomers were faced with the daunting task of finding their niche on the emerging air transport market, defining their strategic and tactical goals and maintaining profitability. The enterprises which had previously handled only local routes were the worst off, being affected to a greater degree by the ups and downs of the national economy and by the whims of the federal and local authorities.

The following photographic album gives an overview of the colourful and varied airline scene in the Russian Federation over the last 15 years. Not all Russian air carriers are covered, of course – it would take a much larger book to do them all justice. Also, though not all of the new airlines established since 1990 have survived, some of the air carriers which are no longer with us are represented, too, since some of them occupied an important place in Russia's airline industry.

Part One deals with the airlines which are 'alive and kicking' as of this writing.

Part Two covers the airlines that are no longer with us – for various reasons. Some air carriers succumbed to economic problems, the notorious Russian bank crisis of 17th August 1998 ('Black Monday') having dealt a crippling blow from which many enterprises never quite recovered. Others have had their operating licences withdrawn dueto unsatisfactory operational standards. The spate of air disasters in Russia in the mid-190s and late 1990s led the Russian Civil Aviation Authority (GSGA – *Gosoodarstvennaya* **sloozh**ba grazh**dahn**skoy avi**ah**tsii, State Civil Aviation Service) to enforce flight safety measures more rigidly and crack down on unscrupulous operators when serious breaches (such as overloading, forged paperwork relating to aircraft parts etc.) were discovered.

For each airline the two-letter International Air Transport Association (IATA) designator and three-letter International Civil Aviation Organisation (ICAO) designator are stated where applicable.

Russian Civil Aircraft Fleet

Airliners	As of 1-1-2003	As of 1-1-2002		Utility aircraft	As of 1-1-2003	As of 1-1-2002
Antonov An-24	250	264		Antonov An-2	1,815	1,897
Ilyushin IL-18	19	27		Antonov An-3	12	–
Ilyushin IL-62/IL-62M	69 *	76		Antonov An-28	35	38
Ilyushin IL-86	73	73		Antonov An-38	6	4
Ilyushin IL-96-300	11	11		Ilyushin IL-103	9	9
Ilyushin IL-114	2	–		Let L-410UVP	90	98
Tupolev Tu-134	238	235		Yakovlev Yak-18T	18	16
Tupolev Tu-154B/B-1/B-2	174	175		TOTAL	1,987	2,062
Tupolev Tu-154M	173	178				
Tupolev Tu-204	13	14		**Helicopters**		
Tupolev Tu-214	3	1		Kamov Ka-26	64	68
Yakovlev Yak-40	314	326		Kamov Ka-32	68	75
Yakovlev Yak-42	81	81		Mil' Mi-2	571	598
Foreign-built aircraft	51	46		Mil' Mi-6	30	31
TOTAL	1,469	1,507		Mil' Mi-8	1,110 ¶	1,124
				Mil' Mi-10K	8	9
Freighters				Mil' Mi-26	55	54
Antonov An-12	76	84		Mil' Mi-34C	8	5
Antonov An-26	165	181		TOTAL	1,914	1,964
Antonov An-30	42	44				
Antonov An-32	11	20				
Antonov An-74	32	24		* including six IL-62s *sans suffixe* and 63 IL-62Ms		
Antonov An-124	20 †	20		† including four An-124s and 16 An-124-100s		
Ilyushin IL-76	181 ‡	179		‡ including 30 IL-76Ts, 110 IL-76TDs, and 41 IL-76MDs		
TOTAL	527	552		¶ including 924 Mi-8Ts/Mi-8Ps and 186 Mi-8MTs *et seq*		

Breakdown of New Indigenous and Foreign-built Aircraft by Carrier

Airliners	As of 1-1-2003	As of 1-1-2002		Business jets	As of 1-1-2003
IL-96-300	11	10		Dassault Falcon 900	2
Aeroflot	6	6		Gazpromavia	2
Domodedovo Airlines	3	3		Dassault Falcon 20C-5	1
Rossiya State Transport Co.	1	1		Meridian	1
Atlant-Soyuz	1	–		Dassault Falcon 20D	3
Tu-204	8	7		Avcom	1
Kavminvodyavia	2	2		Jet 2000	2
KrasAir	2	2		BAe 125-700, BAe 125-800	4
Sibir'	2	2		Avcom	1
Aerofreight (Tu-204C)	2	1		Aero Rent	1
Tu-214	2	1		Meridian	1
Dalavia	2	1		Jet 2000	1
				Cessna 208B Grand Caravan	1
		As of 1-1-2003		Avcom	1
Boeing 737-200, -300, 400, -700		18		Gulfstream G IVSP	1
Aeroflot		10		UTair/Surgutneftegaz	1
Transaero		7		TOTAL	12
SAT		1			
Boeing 767		6		**Helicopters**	
Aeroflot		4		Eurocopter AS 355N Ecureuil	1
Transaero		2		Kogalymavia	1
Boeing 777-200		2		TOTAL	1
Aeroflot		2			
Airbus A310		11			
Aeroflot		11			
Boeing (McDonnell Douglas) DC-10-40F		2			
Aeroflot		2			
TOTAL		39			

The Active Airlines

Abakan-Avia

Seen here on short finals to Moscow-Domodedovo in 2001, IL-76T RA-76504 (c/n 073411330, f/n 0902) is one of the oldest active IL-76s at the time of writing. Note the grey tail and Sobol' trade company badge. RA-76505 and RA-76509 retained basic Aeroflot colours, while RA-76350 was in basic C-Air colours. *Yuriy Kirsanov*

Abakan-Avia [–/ABG], a division of the Sobol' (Sable) trade company, is based in Abakan, the capital of the Republic of Khakasia in Southern Central Siberia. Established in 1992 as one of the two successors of the Krasnoyarsk CAD/Abakan UAD, the airline was initially a pure cargo carrier, operating two Ilyushin IL-76T freighters. In mid-1998 it started scheduled passenger operations with two ex-Armenian Tu-154M medium-haul airliners, though these were later discontinued and the trijets sold. As of mid-2003, the fleet consisted of four Il-76Ts and two IL-76TDs.

Abakan-Avia is involved in humanitarian relief operations. IL-76T RA-76505 (c/n 073411331, f/n 0903) is seen at Zhukovskiy on 24th August 2003 in United Nations World Food Programme markings. *Dmitriy Komissarov*

AeroBratsk

The carrier started life as the Bratsk Air Enterprise, the successor of the East Siberian CAD/Bratsk UAD. The enterprise was subsequently privatised as the Bratsk-Avia Joint-Stock Co, with a 51% state share of the stock, operating domestic passenger scheduled and charter services. In 2000 the airline filed for bankruptcy and was placed under outside management, subsequently reincorporating under the new name AeroBratsk Joint-Stock Co. Currently it operates seven Antonov An-2 utility biplanes, three Mil' Mi-8T utility helicopters, seven Yakovlev Yak-40 feederliners (including two convertible Yak-40Ks) and three Tupolev Tu-154s (one 'B-2 and two 'Ms).

Aeroflot Russian Airlines

For the outside world Aeroflot was represented by the Central Directorate of International Services at Moscow/Sheremet'yevo-2. comprising the 63rd, 64th, 207th, 210th, 216th and 217th Flights which operated the Tu-154, IL-76, Tu-134, IL-62, IL-86 and IL-96-300 respectively. In July 1992 the directorate was transformed into the Aeroflot Russian International Airlines (ARIA, or *Aeroflot – Rosseeyskiye mezhdunarodnyye avialinii*) Joint-Stock Co., with 51% of the shares owned by the state and the rest by the employees and minority shareholders.

At an early stage the airline decided to add Western airliners to its fleet to be operated on the most prestigious routes. In April 1992 the Russian flag carrier took delivery of the first Airbus Industrie A310-300s. In 1993 the air carrier received its first Boeing aircraft (two 767-300ERs).

The crisis of August 1998 affected the Russian airline industry as a whole, though big operators (including ARIA) suffered less damage. Some of the regional airlines operating scheduled services to Moscow, however, were forced to curtail their operations. This led Aeroflot to turn its attention to the domestic market as well, offering services to major regional centres and even striving to take over some of the ailing regional carriers, such as Nizhegorodskiye Airlines and Donavia and turn them into regional branches. Hence in June 2000 the carrier was renamed Aeroflot Russian Airlines, which reflects its status and activities more accurately.

The implementation of ever more stringent regulations concerning noise, pollution and flight safety led Aeroflot to start a large-scale fleet renewal programme which was also aimed at streamlining the fleet.

Given the slow progress in the certification and production of new indigenous aircraft, the decision was taken to buy Western hardware. Thus in April 1998 the airline started taking delivery of Boeing 737-4M0s. In November 2002 Aeroflot signed an order for six Airbus A319-111s and 12 A320-214s, a move widely criticised by the Russian media as yet another stab in the national aircraft industry's back. Deliveries began in November 2003. Concurrently the airline adopted a striking new livery as part of an effort to improve its image.

The current fleet comprises 111 aircraft, including ten IL-76TDs, 14 IL-86s, six IL-96-300s, 14 Tu-134As, 20 Tu-154Ms, 11 A310s, eight A319/A320s, ten Boeing 737-400s, five Boeing 767-300ERs, two Boeing 777-200ERs and two DC-10-40Fs; the IL-62M and Tu-154B-2 have been withdrawn.

Aeroflot Russian Airlines Tu-154M RA-85665 (c/n 89A819) completes its landing run on Moscow-Sheremet'yevo's runway 25L on 26th February 2000. Until 2004 nearly all Aeroflot Tu-154Ms had grey tails supplemented with bold blue trim. The latter was not so much a way of 'livening up a generally uninspiring colour scheme', as Western writers were apt to put it, but rather a measure aimed at disguising the soot stains on the rear fuselage caused by reverse thrust operation – a feature characteristic of the Tu-154M. *Dmitriy Komissarov*

The Ilyushin IL-86 widebody was a valuable asset on Aeroflot's high-density medium-haul routes; in the late 1990s the type was relegated to charter services. This is RA-86058 (c/n 51483203025) in almost unaltered 1973-standard colours, save for the Russian flag and prefix; the vertical tail was later painted grey. *Yuriy Kirsanov*

The IL-62M four-jet airliner, illustrated by grey-tailed RA-86558 (c/n 4952928), a late-production example, was used on Aeroflot's long-haul routes. Only one example (RA-86510) retained the original white tail; several IL-62Ms were aircraft reimported from Germany. Starting in 2000, the type was gradually phased out by Aeroflot. *Yuriy Kirsanov*

Short-haul routes, both domestic and international, were handled by the Tupolev Tu-134A. Again, part of the Tu-134 fleet was formed by reimported aircraft; this is Tu-134AK RA-65623 (c/n (73)49985, f/n 4109) originally built in radar-nosed export configuration for the Polish Air Force (ex '102 Red' No. 2). The white plug in the first full-size window to starboard identifies the aircraft as a Tu-134AK (ie, built as a VIP aircraft); in fact, RA-65623 originally retained its VIP interior before switching to a 68-seat mixed-class layout. Originally ARIA's Tu-134As had white tails and the 'AKs had grey tails; this aircraft departed from the trend by receiving a white tail in 2003. *Yuriy Kirsanov*

Spoilers deployed and the outer engines in reverse thrust mode, IL-76TD RA-76750 (c/n 0083485561, f/n 6501) completes its landing run on runway 25L at Moscow-Sheremet'yevo on 26th February 2000. This aircraft and another ARIA IL-76TD, RA-76476, were·sold to cargo carrier Airstars in 2002.
Dmitriy Komissarov

IL-76TD RA-76479 (c/n 0053460790, f/n 4508) looks (and sounds) magnificent as it approaches its home base on a sunny day. This particular aircraft was used on several occasions for resupplying Soviet research stations in Antarctica, gaining the smart red/white Polar version of Aeroflot's 1973-standard livery for high definition against white backgrounds. The red cheatline and outer wings and black Aeroflot titles/logo remained in post-Soviet times but regrettably the red/white tail was repainted grey, as was the case with the other ARIA IL-76s.
Yuriy Kirsanov

The IL-96-300 took over some of the long-haul routes from the IL-62M, being one of the few Russian aircraft complying with the noise and pollution regulations currently in force. This is RA-96007 (c/n 74393201004) resting between flights on the west side of the apron at Sheremet'yevo-2 in 2000. *Dmitriy Petrochenko*

Aeroflot started introducing Western types into its fleet in 1992, the Airbus Industrie A310 being the first of these. The original five A310-308(ET)s delivered new were French-registered; others, like A310-304(ET) VP-BAF (ex N472GE, c/n 472) seen under tow at Sheremet'yevo-2 on 11th June 1999, are registered in the Bermudas. *Dmitriy Komissarov*

The first of ten Boeing 737-4M0s was delivered to ARIA on 5th May 1998. Here the fourth aircraft delivered in July 1998, VP-BAL (c/n 29204, f/n 3051), taxies in at Sheremet'yevo-2 on 26th February 2000. The blue stripe along the belly is meant to disguise bits of rubber coming off the nosewheel tyres, a perennial problem (usually aircraft with white fuselages tend to compete in who has the dirtiest belly!). *Dmitriy Komissarov*

The airline's fleet includes two Boeing 777-2Q8ERs, the first of which, VP-BAS (c/n 27607, f/n 135) is seen here taxiing at Moscow-Sheremet'yevo in 1998. The new tail colours introduced on the 737/777 gave rise to such crude nicknames as *vzryv na gazoprovode* (explosion on a gas main) and even 'Feuer im Hintern' (fire in the ass)! Note the inscription 'ETOPS' (Extended-range Twin-engine Operations) on the nose gear doors instead of the last three letters of the registration. *Dmitriy Petrochenko*

The long-haul Boeing 767-300ER was added to Aeroflot's fleet in March 1994 to serve the trans-Atlantic routes. The original two Irish-registered 767-3Y0ERs were replaced by four Bermudan-registered 767-36NERs in 1999. The latest example of the type delivered to Aeroflot, Boeing76-38AER VP-BDI (ex N618SH, c/n 29618, f/n 792), was also the first aircraft to be repainted in the Russian flag carrier's new livery introduced in 2003 as part of the effort to enhance the airline's passenger appeal. It is seen here on final approach to Moscow-Sheremet'yevo in October 2003. *Dmitriy Petrochenko*

Resplendent in the airline's new livery, A320-214 VP-BWD (c/n 2093), the fourth Airbus narrowbody delivered to Aeroflot, sits at Sheremet'yevo-2 in November 2003 shortly after delivery. Fortunately the airline chose to retain the familiar logo (albeit in Roman letters now) and winged logo. *Dmitriy Petrochenko*

McDonnell Douglas DC-10-30F(CF) N525MD (c/n 46999, f/n 289) was the first of the type operated by Aeroflot. Two DC-10-40Fs are in service now. *Yuriy Kirsanov*

Aeroflot-Plus

Although this does not show in any way, Tu-134B-3 RA-65694 (c/n (03)63235, f/n 5707) – seen here in the static display of the Civil Aviation-2002 show at Moscow-Domodedovo on 15th August 2002 – is a Tu-134B-3 'Salon' executive jet operated by Aeroflot-Plus. The aircraft previously flew with Latavio Latvian Airlines as YL-LBD. *Dmitriy Komissarov*

A branch called Aeroflot Plus was formed in 1996 for flying business charters. The original plans to acquire two Dassault Falcon 900s had to be abandoned due to high import duties. Instead, two Tu-134AKs were obtained from the parent company, the first service to Shannon being performed in June 1997. Initially the jets were operated when available; flights had to be booked five days in advance, which was inconvenient. In March 1999 Tu-134AK RA-65559 was permanently assigned to Aeroflot Plus after refurbishment with a new 32-seat interior. By January 2001 the fleet was bolstered by Tu-134B-3 'Salon' RA-65694. Both aircraft wear 1973-standard Aeroflot colours.

Aeroflot-Don (ex Donavia)

Donavia Joint-Stock Co. (*Donskiye Avialinii* – Don Airlines) [D9/DNV] was established in August 1993 as the successor of the North Caucasian CAD/Rostov-na-Donu United Air Detachment operating a mix of Tu-154B-2 medium-haul airliners (77th Flight), Tu-134A short-haul twinjets (336th Flight), Yak-40 feederliners (78th Flight) and An-12 freighters. Its activities included domestic and international scheduled passenger services, as well as passenger and cargo charters, including some operated jointly with Lufthansa.

Financial problems forced the carrier to sell off its eleven Yak-40s to start-up MDA Airlines (also based in Rostov-na-Donu) in 1997. In 1998 the airline succumbed to the 17th August bank crisis and filed for bankruptcy protection. Plans for a reunion with the Rostov

The fleet of Donavia included four Tu-134As and two Tu-134AKs. Tu-134A-3 RA-65796 (c/n (03)63150, f/n 5607) was the first to gain the new Aeroflot-Don titles in September 2000. *RART*

The mainstay of Donavia's fleet was formed by the Tu-154B-2 medium-haul trijet, of which seven were on strength. Changing the titles took some time; here, RA-85409 (c/n 80A409), the oldest Tu-154 in the former Donavia's fleet, taxies out under sullen skies at Moscow/Vnukovo-1 on 4th October 2000 for take-off from runway 24, the one most frequently in use due to prevailing winds. The English 'Donavia' titles aft of the forward entry door were extremely unobtrusive. *Dmitriy Komissarov*

airport, from which the carrier was organisationally separated, came to nothing. After a period of negotiations with Aeroflot Russian Airlines it was taken over by the Russian flag carrier as a regional division, changing its name to Aeroflot-Don in April 2000, although the flee continued operating in the old colours for more than a year. Aeroflot has a controlling stake in the airline (51%).

Currently the Aeroflot-Don fleet consists of three Tu-134A-3s, six Tu-154B-2s, three Tu-154Ms (none of the three were inherited from Donavia) and two An-12BPs. The airline operates scheduled passenger network, as well as passenger and cargo charters (mainly to the Middle East and Africa).

Another departure at Moscow/Vnukovo-1 on 5th September 2001 as the carrier's second-youngest Tu-154B-2, RA-85452 (c/n 81A452) – now suitably adorned with Aeroflot-Don titles – taxies out for take-off from runway 20, making the daily flight to Rostov-on-Don. The English titles are as unobtrusive as ever. The huge structure in the background is the new maintenance hangar of the former Vnukovo United Air Detachment; its construction began in the late 1980s but was never finished, the skeleton still standing as a silent reproach for those responsible. Lately Aeroflot-Don has augmented its Tu-154B-2s with three Tu-154Ms purchased from Aeroflot Russian Airlines, Chukotavia and Aviaexpresscruise. *Dmitriy Komissarov*

Aerokuzbass (ex Aerokuznetsk)

That was then. Aerokuznetsk Tu-154B-2 RA-85471 (c/n 81A471) during a turnaround at Moscow-Domodedovo on 3rd November 1998; note the small English titles on the nose. *Dmitriy Komissarov*

Gaining independence in 1991, the Novokuznetsk UFD of the West Siberian CAD (originally founded in 1952) became the Novokuznetsk Air Enterprise, subsequently adopting the name **Aerokuznetsk** [–/NKZ] in 1993. The carrier performed domestic and international passenger scheduled services and cargo charters with Tu-154 medium-haul trijets, Antonov An-24 twin-turboprop regional airliners, An-26 freighters and Mil' Mi-8 utility helicopters. In 1999 the debt-ridden airline was placed in receivership and had to give up part of the fleet (the Antonov turboprops) to pay off debts, subsequently reincorporating under the name Aerokuzbass [–/NKZ]. The current fleet consists of three Mi-8Ts, two Tu-154B-2 and three Tu-154Ms.

This is now. Tu-154M RA-85749 (c/n 92A931) with Aerokuzbass titles on approach to Moscow-Domodedovo in April 2002. *Dmitriy Petrochenko*

Aero Rent

Purchased from the Rossiya State Transport Co. in early 2000, Tu-134AK RA-65557 (c/n (43)66380, f/n 6365) is operated for the Itera Holding Co., a Russian/Kazakh company specialising in petroleum products transportation. Here it is seen at Moscow/Vnukovo-1, its home base, on 22nd March 2001. The other Tu-134AK, RA-65919, had a similar livery but was anonymous until May 2003 when it gained small Aero Rent titles. *Dmitriy Komissarov*

Established in 1995, the Aero Rent Joint-Stock Co. [–/NRO] started operations from Moscow-Vnukovo with initially a single BAe 125-800B biz-jet, operating business charters. Five years later the fleet was expanded by the purchase of two former Russian government Tu-134AK VIP aircraft. The most recent addition to the fleet is a VIP-configured Yak-40, acquired from the Czech Republic. Russian petroleum industry companies are the airline's key customers.

Seen here in the static display of the MAKS-2003 airshow at Zhukovskiy, Yak-40 RA-88306 (c/n 9640651) is operated for Stroytransgaz (a natural gas pipeline construction contractor) in this stylish colour scheme since at least April 2003, hence the Cyrillic 'STG' tail logo. See page 142 for an earlier 'incarnation' of this aircraft. *Dmitriy Komissarov*

Airstars

Established in 2000, Airstars [PL/ASE] – or Aerostarz in Russian – flies cargo charters from Moscow-Domodedovo. Its fleet of freighters (partly leased from other carriers as required) comprises six IL-76TDs, one IL-76T 'Falsie' and one An-12BK. The latest addition to the fleet is two IL-62M airliners converted to combi configuration.

Returned to the lessor since this picture was taken, IL-76TD RA-76812 (c/n 1013407230, f/n 8108) seen at Moscow-Domodedovo on 15th August 2002 was leased from Domodedovo Airlines. Note the white circle on the tail, a leftover from a previous lease to East Line. *Dmitriy Komissarov*

Alania

Seen here on short finals to Moscow-Vnukovo's runway 24 in September 1998, radar-nosed Tu-134AK RA-65616 (c/n 4352206) was Alania Airlines' first aircraft. Originally it flew in the basic red/white colours of the original owner Interflug before gaining this simple but nevertheless appealing livery. Incidentally, most of Alania's fleet consisted of reimported aircraft. This one is ex Komiavia CCCP-65616 No. 2 (the registration previously belonged to a Tu-134K), ex D-AOBF, ex DDR-SCR. The rear door clearly visible in this view is non-functional, as the aircraft has been reconfigured to an 80-seater. *Dmitriy Komissarov*

Alania Leasing Airline [–/OST] was founded in 1996 as the national airline of the Republic of North Osetia (aka Alania). From its base in the North Osetian capital of Vladikavkaz the airline operates scheduled passenger services, originally leasing radar-nosed ex-German Tu-134As and Tu-134AKs from what was then Komiavia as required. A single glass-nosed Tu-134AK (RA-65970) was operated on lease from the Rostov Aircraft Overhaul Plant in 2001-02. That year Alania acquired two Yak-42D short-haul trijets which, together with one Tu-134AK and one Tu-134A, form its present fleet. The airline operates scheduled domestic services, primarily to Moscow-Vnukovo.

Yak-42D RA-42339 (c/n 4520424606267, f/n 0707) was purchased in 2002 from Lithuanian Airlines, with which it flew as LY-AAO. Alania Airlines has two of the type. The white, red and yellow stripes of the tail logo symbolise the national flag of North Osetia (Alania). *Yuriy Kirsanov*

Alliance-Avia

Alliance Avia Yak-40 RA-87530 (c/n 9521241) seen at Samara-Kurumoch in April 2003 shows obvious signs of previous ownership by Tsentr-Avia. It is one of only two aircraft belonging to the carrier, the rest of the fleet being leased. *Dmitriy Petrochenko*

Established in 1996 as a member of ATC Alliance Avia Group, Alliance Avia [–/NZP] based at Zhukovskiy leases the greater part of its fleet from Yamal Airlines. These include four Antonov An-74-200 short take-off and landing transports, a single Tu-134AK reconfigured as a 54-seater and a single 32-seat Yak-40 bought from Tsentr-Avia. All the aircraft retain the basic livery of their former operators with ALLIANCE AVIA titles and A$_A$ tail logo.

Seen at Zhukovskiy on 16th August 1999, An 74-200 RA-74052 (c/n 365.470.98.944, f/n 1702) retains the basic livery of Yamal Airlines; small Yamal titles are actually retained aft of the large portside observation blister. Note that the titles on the port side are in Russian. Two years later the aircraft did not appear to have moved. *Dmitriy Komissarov*

Alrosa (ex Almazy Rossii-Sakha)

Almazy Rossiï – Sakha (Diamonds of Russia–Sakha) [–/DRU], a subsidiary of the identically named diamond mining company based in Mirnyy, Yakutia (the Republic of Sakha), as the successor of the Yakutian CAD/Mirnyy UAD. The latter operated An-24 regional airliners and An-26 transports (190th Flight), IL-76TD freighters (192nd Flight), Mi-8T utility helicopters (402nd Flight), Mi-26T heavy-lift helicopters and An-2 utility biplanes. Part of the Mi-8 fleet was based in

Sanghar and operated by the Sanghar Independent Helicopter Squadron.

Originally the aircraft wore Aeroflot colours with Cyrillic 'Almazy Rossii – Sakha' titles accompanied by two stylised diamonds. By April 2000, however, the airline was rebranded Alrosa (a contraction of the original name) and adopted a stylish colour scheme of its own.

Alrosa operates scheduled domestic scheduled passenger services within and

outside the region, as well as domestic and international cargo charters. The large fleet consists of four IL-76TDs, five Tu-154Ms, five An-24Bs and four An-24RVs, two An-38-100s, two Tu-134B-3s and one Tu-134A, four An-26s, 14 An-2s, 26 Mi-8s and three Mi-26s. The An-38-100s are the youngest and most modern aircraft in the fleet, being acquired as a replacement for the ageing An-24s.

'Diamonds are forever.' Resplendent in the new stylish livery adopted by the carrier in 2000 when Almazy Rossiï – Sakha was rebranded Alrosa, IL-76TD RA-76360 (c/n 1033414492, f/n 8803) completes its landing run at Moscow-Domodedovo, one of its regular destinations. In June 1999 this aircraft was operated by Samara Airlines on lease from Almazy Rossiï – Sakha. The tail logo represents the Republic of Sakha's status as a diamond-rich region. *Yuriy Kirsanov*

Though Almazy Rossiï – Sakha had long operated feeder services with An-24s and Mi-8s, it was not until 1999 that Tu-154M medium-haul airliners were acquired. By 2002 the fleet had grown to five. Here, RA-85675 (c/n 90A835), a former Russian Government (Rossiya State Transport Co.) VIP aircraft, undergoes maintenance at Moscow/Vnukovo-1 on 18th June 2002. *Dmitriy Komissarov*

IL-76TD RA-76357 (c/n 1033414467, f/n 8707) illustrates the old livery of Almazy Rossiï – Sakha, actually nothing more than basic Aeroflot colours with the same two stylised diamonds (albeit in a much more modest presentation) painted on with the old long titles. This aircraft was the first IL-76 to be repainted in the new Alrosa colours in April 2000. *Yuriy Kirsanov*

Alrosa-Avia

Unless you know it, you'll never guess when looking from this angle that RA-65907 (c/n (33)63996, f/n 6333) is a Tu-134AK and not a regular Tu-134A – the galley window immediately aft of the service door is missing, as is the white 'plug' in the first full-size window to starboard! In Soviet times this aircraft was a testbed for the Mikoyan MiG-29M fighter's fire control radar. After that it flew in basic Aeroflot colours with Alrosa-Avia titles/logo until repainted in this new livery patterned on that of the parent company, Alrosa. It is seen at Moscow/Vnukovo-1 on 6th May 2003. *Dmitriy Komissarov*

Alrosa-Avia [–/LRO], the Moscow subsidiary of Almazy Rossiï – Sakha, was established in 1993, initially operating a single Tu-134AK from Zhukovskiy and Moscow-Vnukovo. A second example, Tu-134B-3 'Salon' RA-65693, was bought from Aviaenergo in May 2001. Additionally, Alrosa-Avia operated a Mil' Mi-8 helicopter and an Antonov An-26 transport.

Amur Airlines

Based in Khabarovsk in the Russian Far East, Amur Airlines established in 1993 is the flying division of the Amur Gold Mining Company (*Artel' starateley Amur*). Its small but varied fleet included Mil' Mi-2 and Mi-8T utility helicopters, Antonov An-2 utility biplanes, An-24RV airliners (no longer operated as of this writing) and An-26B transports.

An-24RV RA-46612 (c/n 37308609), a former Voronezhavia aircraft, taxies out for take-off at Khabarovsk-Novyy in 2002, illustrating the restrained but attractive livery of Amur Airlines The aircraft had been sold by the spring of 2003. *Dmitriy Petrochenko*

Amur Airlines An-26B RA-26048 (c/n 10901) sits on a wet apron at Khabarovsk-Novyy in 2002, with an An-24 and a further An-26 in the colours of the same airline visible beyond. *Dmitriy Petrochenko*

Antex-Polus

Founded in 1998, Antex-Polus Joint-Stock Co. [–/AKP] based at Yermolino, Moscow Region, is the successor of the defunct Yermolino Airlines, operating the former carrier's fleet of four An-12 transports, one An-2 and one Tu-134AK. The airline also occasionally operated Mil' Mi-8 helicopters leased as required.

Seen parked in front of the unfinished maintenance hangar at Moscow/Vnukovo-1 on 6th May 2003, Tu-134AK RA-65908 (c/n (23)63870, f/n 6307) is one of the three known examples to lack the galley window to starboard and the white 'plug' in the first first full-size window (which makes them unidentifiable as Tu-134AKs unless you know it). The aircraft wears a rather gaudy 'genetically modified zebra' colour scheme with a very unobtrusive Antex-Polus logo on the nose. *Dmitriy Komissarov*

Astrakhan Airlines

Astrakhan' Airlines (Astrakhanskiye Avialinii) [OB/ASZ] were established in 1994 as the successor of the North Caucasian CAD/Astrakhan' United Flight Detachment/110th Flight based at Narimanovo airport. Currently the government owns no more than 25.5% of the airline's stock; 51% is owned by the employees and the rest by other investors.

The carrier has scheduled services to Moscow-Domodedovo, Yekaterinburg, Yerevan, Baku and Sochi/Adler, as well as charter flights to Istanbul, Cairo, Rimini, Antalya, Rhodes and the UAE.

As of mid-1999 Astrakhan' Airlines operated two Yak-42Ds, five Tu-134A-3s, six An-24Bs/RVs, one Mi-8T, seven An-2s and eleven Ka-26 utility helicopters. By 2003, however, the Yak-42s, the An-2s, the Ka-26s and half the An-24 fleet had been disposed of.

The Tu-134A makes up the mainstay of Astrakhan' Airlines' fleet. Here, RA-65055 (c/n (73)49856, f/n 3906) is seen taxiing out for take-off at Moscow-Domodedovo on 18th October 1998 past two of the resident Domodedovo Civil Aviation Production Association IL-62Ms. *Dmitriy Komissarov*

Atlant-Soyuz

Since 1998 Atlant-Soyuz is known as 'the Moscow Government airline' because the Moscow Government has a stake in it; hence some Atlant-Soyuz aircraft wear additional Cyrillic Aviakompaniya pravitel'stva Moskvy titles, much to the amusement of spotters. One of them is IL-86 RA-86139 (c/n 51483210098), seen here 'firing up' at Moscow/Sheremet'yevo-2 on 18th September 1998. Note the Moscow city crest with St. George and the dragon ahead of the titles. *Dmitriy Komissarov*

Atlant-Soyuz Airlines [3G/AYZ] established on 8th June 1993 operate scheduled and charter passenger and cargo services from Moscow/Sheremet'yevo-2, Moscow-Domodedovo and Chkalovskaya AB (until the use of the latter as a civil airport was banned after the crash of a Roos' JSC IL-76 in July 2001). The airline mostly operates aircraft leased from other carriers and the Russian, Belorussian and Ukrainian air forces as required; hence the fleet changes constantly and keeping track of it is all but impossible. Over the years the airline has operated such varied types as the IL-18D, IL-62M, Tu-134AK and Tu-154B-2 airliners (leased from the Russian Air Force and operated in Aeroflot colours), the IL-86 wide-

Seen here taxiing at Moscow/Sheremet'yevo-2 in May 2001, IL-86 EK-86117 (c/n 51483209085) was leased from Armenian Airlines in the summer of 1999. The aircraft wore AAL's current.
Dmitriy Petrochenko

IL-76TD EW-76710 (c/n 0063473182, f/n 5505) – again with Aviakompaniya pravitel'stva Moskvy subtitles – was leased from the Transaviaexport cargo airline (the commercial division of the Belorussian Air Force), as the tail colours reveal. It is seen here in somewhat incomplete condition at Zhukovskiy on 23rd September 1999. This aircraft is a converted IL-76MD that has had the tail gunner's station replaced by a 'commercial' tailcone.
Dmitriy Komissarov

Displaying only Atlant-Soyuz titles, recently overhauled IL-76TD RA-76798 (c/n 1003403063, f/n 7706) leased from Samara Airlines is being unloaded at Moscow/Vnukovo-1 on 5th September 2001. The airline's IL-76s display a variety of markings; for instance, IL-76TD EW-78801 leased from Transaviaexport in 1998 had basic Aeroflot colours with Atlant-Soyuz titles and the 'winged a' tail logo, while RA-76401 displayed the Moscow city crest on the tail. *Dmitriy Komissarov*

body, An-12 and IL-76TD freighters. As of this writing, the airline has an all-Ilyushin fleet of 12 IL-76s, two IL-86s and a single IL-96-300 used as a freighter.

Over the years Atlant-Soyuz has established a strong position on the air cargo market, ranking second only to Aeroflot Russian Airlines in this field in 1998. The air-line does a lot of business on the lucrative routes to Chin a (the airline's main market since 1998) and the United Arab Emirates; cargo carriage accounted for 74% of the total revenue in 2000. The carrier also operates a good deal of passenger charters, having established a travel agency of its own in 1997.

Atlant-Soyuz is the launch customer for two new Russian commercial aircraft – the IL-96-400T freighter and the recently certificated 120-seat Tu-334-100 short/medium-haul airliner, of which two and five respectively are on order for 2004-05. Additionally, six brand-new An-124-100 'big lifters' are due for delivery in 2004.

Another variation on the theme. IL-76TD RA-76445 (c/n 1023410330, f/n 8403) leased from Gazpromavia in 2001 (and seen here at Moscow-Domodedovo in company with Aram Air IL-76TEP-RAM) retained full Gazpromavia colours with the addition of Atlant-Soyuz titles – incidentally, applied directly over the Russian flag on the nose. By May 2003 the aircraft had been returned to the lessor and the additional titles had been removed. *Yuriy Kirsanov*

Atran (ex Aviatrans)

An-12B RA-93915 (c/n 4342105) in the early colours of Aviatrans seen on approach to Moscow-Domodedovo in 1998. Many of the airline's aircraft wore non-standard registrations. The blue spinner tips are probably a leftover from the aircraft's Air Force days when it had overt military markings. *Yuriy Kirsanov*

In 1992 the Moscow UFD of the 'Transport Aviation' Production Association, a division of the Ministry of Aircraft Industry (MAP – *Ministerstvo aviatsionnoy promyshlennosti*) based at Moscow-Domodedovo and Moscow-Myachkovo was transformed into Aviatrans Cargo Airlines [V8/VAS]. On 1st January 1997 the airline changed its name to Atran – Aviatrans Cargo Airlines. Over the years Aviatrans/Atran has operated eight An-12s, eight IL-76s, six An-26s and three An-32s, including several ex-Iraqi and ex-Peruvian aircraft. Two An-26s, seven An-12s and two IL-76TDs are in service as of this writing.

An-26 RA-26218 (ex CCCP-26218, ex Peruvian Air Force FAP-363, c/n 5408) a second before touching down on runway 14L at Moscow-Domodedovo, its home base. Sister ship RA-27210 was likewise a former Peruvian machine (ex FAP-379). *Yuriy Kirsanov*

IL-76T RA-76789 (ex CCCP-76789, ex Iraqi Airways YI-ALP, c/n 0013433999, f/n 2510) on short finals to Moscow-Domodedovo. Actually this is what the authors call an IL-76T 'Falsie' – ie, despite the 'IL-76T' nose titles the aircraft has a tail gunner's station identifying it as an IL-76M. Note that the aircraft has been demilitarised, the UKU-9K-502-I tail turret being deleted and replaced with a dished fairing in accordance with its civil status. *Yuriy Kirsanov*

Two An-12BPs in the current livery of Atran with the double cheatline sit on the eastern side of the apron at Moscow-Domodedovo on 17th August 2002, with RA-93913 (c/n 4342609) nearest. The aircraft has been partially demilitarised (the DB-65U tail turret is still there but the tail gunner's station windows have been overpainted; the c/n is erroneously painted on the port side of the tail as 3442609. RA-93912 (c/n 4341709) in the background carries an 'Operated for Miras Air' sticker. *Dmitriy Komissarov*

An-26B RA-26595 (c/n 13401), seen at Moscow-Domodedovo on 17th August 2002, is one of two remaining on strength with Atran as of this writing. Unusually, the titles visible under the engine nacelle are Cyrillic (ATPAH instead of ATRAN).
Dmitriy Komissarov

Atruvera

Displaying recently reapplied Atruvera markings after return from a lease to Sukhoi, IL-76TD 'Falsie' RA-76659 (c/n 0053463908, f/n 4807) is unloaded at Moscow/Vnukovo-1 on 29th May 2000. It is an Afghan War veteran, as revealed by the APP-50 flare dispenser housings in the main gear fairings. The aircraft is not demilitarised yet but the inert gas generator in the starboard main gear fairing is faired over. *Dmitriy Komissarov*

Atruvera Air Transport Company [–/AUV], a specialised cargo airline, operates four IL-76TD 'Falsies', one 'true' IL-76TD and three Mil' Mi-26 heavy-lift helicopters from St. Petersburg-Pulkovo and Moscow-Domodedovo (operations from Zhukovskiy were discontinued in 2001). Atruvera is an acronym for **a**via**trahns**portnyye **u**sloo**g**i **v** *Y***e***v***rop**e i **Ah***zii* – air transport services in Europe and Asia. Originally the airline leased IL-76MDs from the Russian Air Force as required.

Avcom

Established in 1992 when free enterprise started booming in Russia, Avcom [J6/AOC] is a specialised business charter operator (the name is a contraction of 'avia-tion, commercial'). From its base at Moscow/Sheremet'yevo-1 (where a general aviation terminal was constructed in the late 1990s) it operated such varied types as the Tu-134AK/Tu-134A 'Salon'/Tu-134B 'Salon', BAe 125-700, Dassault Falcon 20B, Yak-40 'Salon' and Yak-142, though part of the fleet was later sold to LUKoil-Avia (see page 77).

RA02800, the seventh production BAe 125-700 and the first of the type operated in Russia (ex G-BUNL, ex G-5-721, c/n 257007), taxies at Moscow-Sheremet'yevo in 1993. As the titles and logo show, it was operated for the Tomskneft' oil company. The aircraft was sold to the USA, becoming N257TH on 18th August 1999. *Yuriy Kirsanov*

Until recently Avcom had no standard livery of its own, and every aircraft in the fleet was painted differently. This is RA-65701, a refitted Tu-134B 'Salon' (ex Baltic Express Line YL-LBI, c/n (03)63365, f/n 5710) placed on the Russian register on 16th November 2001; the aircraft has a curved red/blue cheatline. *Yuriy Kirsanov*

Tu-134A-3 'Salon' RA-65079 (ex LY-ASK, c/n (73)60054, f/n 4206) bought from Tulpar in 2001 (see page 117) introduced what looks set to be the new fleetwide standard with red and dark blue trim. Yak-40 'Salon 2nd Class' RA-87977 (ex Czech government OK-BYH, c/n 9321128) wears the same livery. *Yuriy Kirsanov*

The latest Western biz-jet operated by Avcom, BAe 125-700B RA-02850 (c/n 257112) retains the colour scheme it wore when it was G-SVLB. It is seen here in the static park of the Civil Aviation-2002 airshow at Moscow-Domodedovo on 15th August 2002. *Dmitriy Komissarov*

Aviaenergo

Aviaenergo [7U/ERG] was established in 1994 as the Zhukovskiy-based flying division of the United Energy System of Russia Joint-Stock Co. ('*Yedinaya energhetich-eskaya sistema Rossii*', the electric power monopoly). Initially operating a single IL-76TD freighter (a second example was added in 1996), the carrier steadily expanded its fleet, moving into the passenger charter market by acquiring three Tu-154Ms in 1994-95. A 36-seat Tu-134B-3

'Salon' and a Yak-40 'Salon 2nd Class' were bought in 1996. Long-haul passenger operations were catered for by two IL-62Ms, one of which was outfitted as the VIP jet of Anatoliy Chubaïs, the notorious chief of the United Energy System of Russia JSC. Other types operated included Mi-8T utility helicopters and a single An-74 STOL transport.

Aviaenergo operates domestic and international cargo and passenger charters. In 1997-99 it had an agreement with Aeroflot

Russian International Airlines, performing scheduled services on behalf of the Russian flag carrier; during the same period the two IL-76s were jointly operated with East Line.

Unfortunately Aviaenergo's original livery gave way to steadily duller colour schemes, the characteristic yellow/green/ red bands on the fuselage being eliminated because they looked too much like the Lithuanian flag. The current fleet comprises two IL-62Ms, one Tu-134AK (bought from from the Russian Air Force as a replacement for the Tu-134B which had been sold), two Tu-154Ms and one IL-76TD which is on lease to Volga-Dnepr Airlines. The main operating base has switched to Moscow-Sheremet'yevo.

Aviaenergo's first aircraft, IL-76TD RA-76843 (c/n 1033418584, f/n 9006) at its home base in Zhukovskiy in 1995, displaying the airline's attractive original livery. The aircraft was sold to Cen-Sad in 2002 as 5A-DKS. *RART*

RA-85797 (c/n 94A981), Aviaenergo's first Tu-154M, seen during a turnaround at Stockholm-Arlanda on 15th August 1997 while making an intermediate stop during a Moscow-Copenhagen-Stockholm-Moscow service operated on behalf of Aeroflot. Note the additional 'From Aeroflot' titles. *Dmitriy Komissarov*

Passenger-configured IL-62M RA-86130 (c/n 3255333) in its original colour scheme – and likewise sporting additional 'From Aeroflot' titles beneath the forward entry door – is towed at Moscow/Sheremet'yevo-2 on 11th June 1999. Note the IL-62's trademark feature, the castoring twin-wheel support under the tail which is extended on the ground to prevent the machine from falling over backwards.
Dmitriy Komissarov

Tu-134B-3 RA-65693 (ex Latavio latvian Airlines YL-LBC, c/n (03)63221, f/n 5706) parked at Moscow/Sheremet'yevo-1 in 1998 following its return from lease to Air Vita; the multi-coloured stripes were not reinstated and the 'Electric Eagle' tail logo is toned down a bit. Despite the the white 'plug' in the first first full-size window, this aircraft does not have a rear entry door to port. In May 2001 RA-65693 was sold to Alrosa-Avia. *RART*

RA-85809 (c/n 94A985), the youngest of Aviaenergo's Tu-154Ms, in the carrier's latest livery which was introduced on Tu-134AK .RA-65962 in March 2001.
S. and D. Komissarov collection

This view of RA-85797 at a later date makes an interesting comparison with that on page 26. Here the aircraft is pictured in an interim colour scheme at Moscow/Vnukovo-1 on 22nd March 2001 (probably after receiving attention at the Vnukovo Aircraft Overhaul Plant, since Aviaenergo does not operate from Vnukovo). The affiliation with Aeroflot has come to an end. In this version of the Aviaenergo livery Cyrillic 'RAO YeES Rossiï' (United Energy Systems of Russia JSC) titles are still carried on the nose; they were eliminated in the latest livery. Two stored former Vnukovo Airlines Tu-154B-2s are visible beyond. *Dmitriy Komissarov*

IL-62M 'Salon' RA-86583 (c/n 1356851) wore this unimposing all-white livery when it was added to the fleet in July 1996. This is the VIP aircraft of Anatoliy Chubaïs, one of Russia's best-known tycoons, and hence has been dubbed *Chubaïsolyot* ('the Chubaïs Flyer). Incidentally, the airline's name (written in Cyrillic characters) has proved something of a problem to foreigners who have corrupted it as 'Aviaznergo' and even 'Avianegro'! *Yuriy Kirsanov*

Aviaexpresscruise

Established in 1993, the charter carrier Aviaexpresscruise [E6/BKS] based at Moscow-Vnukovo operated a variety of aircraft, many of which were leased from other carriers as required. These included four Tu-134As, one Tu-134B-3, at least one Tu-154B-2, five Tu-154Ms (mostly ex-Chinese aircraft), four Yak-40s and, more recently, two Yak-42Ds operated jointly with the Georgian airline Adjaria based in Batumi.

Opposite page, bottom: Tu-154B-2 RA-85604 (c/n 84A604) leased from Orenburg Airlines in 1998 even retains the lessor's logo aft of the flight deck. The rendering of the Aviaexpresscruise titles is noteworthy (compare with the later version worn by the other aircraft illustrated here); the meaning of the winged 'Mak' badge ahead of the titles remains unknown. Previously CCCP-85604 was a Tu-154B-2 'Salon' VIP aircraft outfitted with special communications equipment and adorned with 'Sovetskiy Soyuz' (Soviet Union) titles; it was this aircraft which took Mikhail S. Gorbachov to Oslo in May 1991 to receive the Nobel Peace Prize. *Yuriy Kirsanov*

Right: Seen here as it completes its landing roll on Moscow-Vnukovo's runway 24, passing the intersection with runway 02/20, Tu-134A-3 RA-65117 (c/n (83)60450, f/n 4606) was leased from Orenburg Airlines in 2000-2002. The blue-painted rudder identifies it as an Orenburg Airlines aircraft; note the winged AEC logo ahead of the entry door. *Yuriy Kirsanov*

Above: Seen here taxiing at Moscow/Sheremet'-yevo-1, Yak-40K RA-87924 (c/n 9731555) was operated by Aviaexpresscruise in the summer of 2001 in this all-white livery with the original version of the logo (which, true enough, was also worn by the Tu-154Ms operated in recent times). The cargo door is not visible in this view. *Dmitriy Petrochenko*

Right: Seen basking in the sun on a snow-covered apron at Moscow/Vnukovo-1 on 22nd March 2001, Tu-134B-3 RA-65569 (c/n (03)63340, f/n 5807) is ex Sukhumi Airlines 4L-AAB bought in February 2000. The dark blue/white colour scheme is patterned on that of Lat-Charter with which the aircraft flew as YL-LBH; since it was originally CCCP-65700 with Aeroflot, it really should have become RA-65700. In September 2001 this aircraft was sold to Daghestan Airlines. *Dmitriy Komissarov*

Seen resting between flights in front of the terminal at Moscow/Vnukovo-1 on 6th May 2001, Yak-42D 4L-AAR (ex China General Aviation B-2751, c/n 4520423116650, f/n 0314) belongs to the Batumi-based airline Adjaria (not to be confused with an earlier operator called Adjarian Airlines!) but is regularly operated under Aviaexpresscruise's E6 flight code, serving the daily flight to Batumi; so is sister ship 4L-AAM (ex B-2754, c/n 4520423116579, f/n 0613). The corporate-style colour scheme and the complete lack of titles/logos has kept spotters guessing as to who owns these aircraft. *Dmitriy Komissarov*

Avial'-NV

Avial' Aviation Co. Ltd. [–/RLC] was set up on 21st March 1991 and began operations on 24th December 1992. It operates cargo charters charter flights throughout Russia, the CIS and the Middle East from Moscow-Domodedovo and Sheremet'yevo-1 with a fleet of An-12s, occasionally leasing IL-76TDs. In 2000 the name was changed to Avial'-NV [–/NVI]. Two years later the airline moved into the passenger airline market, adding three An-28 feederliners to its fleet which currently also includes six An-12s. RA-11345 (c/n 401801), a demilitarised An-12B, is illustrated here.

Avialinii 400

IL-76TD RA-76483 (c/n 0063468042, f/n 5201) begins its landing gear retraction sequence as it takes off from Moscow-Domodedovo. Though in full Avialinii 400 colours, the aircraft was leased to Atlant-Soyuz when the picture was taken. *Yuriy Kirsanov*

Opposite page, bottom: Still in basic Bashkirian Airlines livery, Tu-154M RA-85847 (ex CSA Czech Airlines OK-TCD, c/n 88A792) taxies in at Moscow/Vnukovo-1 on 5th September 2001. *Dmitriy Komissarov*

Avialinii Chetyresto (Airlines 400) [–/VAZ], the flying division of Aircraft Overhaul Plant No. 400 at Moscow-Vnukovo, incorporated in 1999. Starting out with a single IL-76TD in 2000, it has since expanded its fleet to three IL-76TDs (all ex-Magadanavialeasing), four Tu-154Ms and a single Tu-134AK. In addition to flying passenger and cargo charters on its own, the airline readily leases its aircraft to other operators; for instance, Tu-154Ms RA-65650 and RA-65680 have been operated by Bulgarian Air Charter as LZ-LCI and LZ-LCE respectively, while RA-85653 was leased to Tomskneftegaz.

Aviast

Established in 1992, the Aviast Joint-Stock Co. [–/VVA] operated a total of six IL-76TDs, leasing or buying most of them from Sakha Avia. Most of these aircraft – RA-76485, RA-76486, RA-76487 and RA-76797 – were 'true' IL-76TDs; RA-76754 leased from Atran was a 'Falsie'. RA-76849 (depicted here taxiing at Moscow-Domodedovo) is an unusual bird, however, being nothing less than a converted and reregistered 'true' IL-76MD which previously flew with the Ukrainian airline Hoseba (ex UR-86921, c/n 0023440161, f/n 3001); the conversion was undertaken in 1998. Originally the IL-76s wore basic Aeroflot colours with Aviast titles/logo; a more stylish livery was adopted by April 2002 (see next page). *Yuriy Kirsanov*

The other major type operated by Aviast is the An-12.Three of the type are operated; RA-11962 (ex Trans Aero Samara, c/n 5343007) and RA-69314 bought from Aviastar in 2001 (see below) wear full colours, while RA-11756 has a simpler grey/white colour scheme. A single Yak-40, RA-87800, is also operated. *Yuriy Kirsanov*

Aviastar

The Aviastar Joint-Stock Co˛ (formerly the Ul'yanovsk Aircraft Production Complex) producing the An-124 Ruslan heavy transport and the Tu-204 medium-haul air-liner has a flying division of the same name [–/FUE] performing domestic and international cargo and passenger charters. The airline's fleet included two An-12BPs (both subsequently sold), three An-26s (two of which are navaids calibration aircraft) and two Yak-40 'Salons'. Here, An-12BP RA-69314 (c/n 5343004) is seen at Moscow-Domodedovo on 3rd November 1998. *Dmitriy Komissarov*

Yak-40 'Salon 2nd Class' RA-87244 (c/n 9531243) in 1994-standard colours. By 2000 the colour scheme had been changed to feature the intertwined letters 'AS' by way of a tail logo instead of the aircraft type which was boldly marked on the tail, as illustrated here. *Yuriy Kirsanov*

AVL Arkhangel'sk Airlines

Established in 1991, this is one of the oldest post-Soviet air carriers. AVL (Arkhangel'skiye vozdooshnyye linïi – Arkhangel'sk Air Lines) is the former Arkhangel'sk CAD/1st Arkhangel'sk UAD based at Talagi airport and flying An-24s, An-26s (392nd Flight), Tu-134As (312th Flight) and Tu-154s.

The airline operates scheduled and charter passenger and cargo services both in and outside the CIS. Moscow, St. Petersburg and Murmansk are the main destinations in Russia; flights to the southern regions of Russia, the Urals and Western Siberia are added in the summer season. Outside the CIS, AVL operated scheduled flights to Rovaniemi (Finland), Tromsö (Norway) and Luleå (Sweden), plus charters to Antalya, Athens and Saloniki.

The current fleet consists of three An-24RVs, ten An-26s/An-26Bs, seven Tu-134A/A-3s and five Tu-154B-2s. Plans for fleet renewal (including the purchase of three IL-114 regional turboprops with delivery initially planned for 1997) have been put on hold after the 1998 bank crisis.

In addition to regular transport duties, AVL used the An-26 for firefighting (in An-26P waterbomber guise) and for ice patrol and fishery reconnaissance (as the An-26BRL equipped with a side-looking radar). Here, RA-26615 (c/n 5001) seen on approach to Moscow-Sheremet'yevo illustrates the livery worn in the early 1990s – Aeroflot colours augmented by an Arkhangel'skiye vozdooshnyye linïi badge on the nose. Interestingly, the aircraft lacks the navigator's blister, though it is not an An-26B. *Yuriy Kirsanov*

For the greater part of the 1990s, AVL Arkhangel'sk Airlines aircraft wore either Aeroflot colours (with or without titles) or a rather nondescript livery with a blue tail on which the white letters АВЛ (AVL in Cyrillic) were painted; the latter livery gave rise to scornful remarks from some Western observers that 'they did not have enough paint for the titles'. In 1997, however, the detractors were put to shame when AVL introduced this stunning colour scheme featuring 'Northern lights' tail trim and bold red titles. Here, An-24RV RA-46651 (c/n 47309202) caught by the camera on short finals to Moscow-Sheremet'yevo emphasises the ability of modern airline liveries to give old aircraft a completely new look. Note the small white Aeroflot titles on the centre fuselage (AVL had a code-sharing agreement with Aeroflot). *Yuriy Kirsanov*

Tu-134A-3 RA-65103 (c/n (83)60297, f/n 4410), like-wise photographed on final approach to Moscow-Sheremet'yevo in the new livery, is named *Nar'yan-Mar* after a city in the Arkhangel'sk Region (the name is carried beneath the АВЛ nose titles).
Yuriy Kirsanov

Tu-134A-3 RA-65066 (c/n (73)49898, f/n 4008) was the first aircraft to adopt the airline's new look and thus has a somewhat non-standard livery – compare with RA-65103 above. The characteristic smutty stripes on the Tu-134's engine nacelles along the nacelle/cowling joint are caused by oil leaking from under the accessory gearbox and decomposing on the hot engine casing. *Yuriy Kirsanov*

Bashkirian Airlines

BAL Bashkirian Airlines (*Bashkirskiye Avi-alinii*) [V9/BTC] were founded in 1991 as the Volga CAD/Ufa UAD, a major Aeroflot unit operating An-24 regional airliners (415th Flight), Tu-134A short-haul jets and Tu-154B-2/Tu-154M medium-haul jets (282nd Flight) and Mi-8 helicopters. In 1999 BAL streamlined their fleet by forming two divisions, **Trahns**portnaya Aviahtsiya Bashkorto**stana** (Bashkirian Cargo Aviation), which operated four An-74 freighters, and **Ma**laya Aviahtsiya Bashkor-to**stana** (Bashkirian Light Aviation), which took over operation of 70 utility aircraft – An-2 biplanes and assorted choppers, including four brand-new Mi-34S light helicopters. Several aircraft were used as VIP jets in support of the republic's government.

Among Russia's major airlines BAL was one of the hardest hit by the 1998 crisis but did its best to stay afloat. The large fleet had to be streamlined due to excess capacity, the surviving Tu-154B-2s, the utility aircraft and most of the An-24s being placed in storage. Nevertheless the carrier has managed to make a recovery.

Today BAL operates scheduled passenger and cargo services within the CIS, as well as passenger charters to Asia, Europe and North Africa. The current fleet comprises nine Tu-154Ms (seven of which are reimported aircraft), three Tu-134As, three An-74s, the last remaining An-24RV, six Mi-8Ts and three Mi-34Ss.

RA-85318 (c/n 78A318) taxies at Moscow-Domodedovo after arriving on the daily flight from Ufa. Originally part of the fleet sported nothing more than Bashkirskiye Avialinii titles. *Yuriy Kirsanov*

Some Tu-154B-2s, like RA-85347 (c/n 79A347) seen on the western apron at Moscow-Domodedovo during a quick turnaround on 18th October 1998, sported this hybrid livery with a blue tail. A few, like RA-85349, did gain full BAL colours (see overleaf). The airline's logo is a stylised bee because Bashkiria is a purveyor of high-quality honey. *Dmitriy Komissarov*

Although the Tu-154B-2 had been phased out by the airline by 2002, RA-85450 (c/n 80A450) was leased from Perm' Airlines in July 2002 after the crash of Tu-154M RA-85816, wearing this non-standard all-white colour scheme. It was returned to the lessor in late 2003. *Dmitriy Petrochenko*

The Tu-154M is the mainstay of BAL's current fleet. Here, RA-85816 (c/n 95A1006), one of the last off the line, takes off from runway 32L at Moscow-Domodedovo, showing off full BAL colours. In 1999-2000 this aircraft was leased to the Pakistani carrier Shaheen Airlines. Tragically, on 2nd July 2002 RA-85816 collided with DHL Aviation Boeing 757-23APF A9C-DHL near Überlingen, Germany, due to a Swiss air traffic controller's error with the tragic death of all aboard. *Yuriy Kirsanov*

Tu-134A-3 RA-65026 (c/n (63)48470, f/n 3602) basks in the sun at Moscow-Domodedovo on 18th November 1998. By 2003 this aircraft had been retired. *Dmitriy Komissarov*

An-24B RA-46568 (c/n 87304709) on short finals to Moscow-Domodedovo. It was retired in Ufa in 1998. *Yuriy Kirsanov*

Belgorod Air Enterprise

Based in Belgorod in Central Russia's bread belt, the Belgorod Air Enterprise (formerly the Central Regions CAD/ Belgorod UAD) operates eight Yak-40 trijets, as well as An-2 biplanes and Ka-26 helicopters performing crop-spraying work.

Yak-40 'Salon 2nd Class' RA-87993 (c/n 9541744) in a special colour scheme to support the local Belogor'ye Volleyball Club, pictured at Moscow/ Vnukovo-1 on 6th May 2003. *Dmitriy Komissarov*

Buryatia Airlines

Bought in March 1997, Tu-154M RA-85827 (c/n 86A745) was ex LOT Polish Airlines SP-LCC. It is seen here in full Buryatia Airlines colours; the blue/white/yellow cheatline symbolises the Buryat national flag. The aircraft was leased to East Line in 1998 and subsequently sold to Enkor. The airline's first Tu-154M, RA-85800 (now belonging to Pulkovo Avia), had a similar colour scheme but wore large 'MOTOM' titles. *Yuriy Kirsanov*

Established in 1993 under the trading name Motom (a Buryat word of unknown meaning) and then renamed Buryatia Airlines [U4/BUT], the carrier was the successor of the East Siberian CAD/Ulan-Ude United Air Detachment comprising the 138th Flight (operating An-2s, An-24s and An-26s) and the 183rd Flight operating Mi-2 and Mi-8 helicopters. In 2001 the name was changed again to Bural [U4/BUN] (a contraction of *Buryatskiye avialinii*).

From its base at Ulan-Ude/Mookhino, the principal airport of the republic's capital) the airline performs regional passenger services with three An-24s (out of an original ten), as well as utility work with four Mi-2s (out of the original six), four An-2s (out of the original 20) and seven Mi-8s (out of the original 12). The three Tu-154Ms bought in 1994-97 have been sold, as have the two An-26 freighters.

Bylina

Bylina (the word *bylina* means 'old legend' or 'saga') is a business charter operator. Starting life in early 1998, the carrier initially flew a single Yak-40 'Salon 2nd Class' (RA-87342) leased from Tatarstan Airlines/ Bugul'ma Air Enterprise, moving its operations base from Moscow-Bykovo to Moscow/Vnukovo-1 in 1999.

A curious aspect of this carrier is that each aircraft wore a totally different colour scheme. Yak-40 RA-87440 (c/n 9431635) pictured above at Moscow/Vnukovo-1 on 18th February 2002 displays obvious signs of previous ownership by AeroTeks, only the tail colours having been changed. RA-87342 had a much more stylish red/white/gold colour scheme. *Dmitriy Komissarov*

Close-up of the tail logo depicting a stylised knight on horseback with shield and flying cloak. *Dmitriy Komissarov*

Although Bylina has not been listed in airline fleet list reference books for years, here is evidence that the airline is alive and kicking! Yak-40 RA-88168 (c/n 9610647, a former Komiavia aircraft pictured in front of the control tower at Moscow-Vnukovo on 18th June 2002 wears a predominantly livery with a 'lightning bolt' cheatline in Russian flag colours. Note how the cheatline continues across the centre engine's thrust reverser doors; these are normally left unpainted. *Dmitriy Komissarov*

Cheboksary Air Enterprise

Yuriy Kirsanov

The Cheboksary Air Enterprise [–/CBK] emerged in the early 1990s as the successor of the Volga CAD/Cheboksary UFD, intending to become the new national air carrier of the Chuvashian Republic. The carrier's activities included domestic passen-ger scheduled flights/charters and utility tasks, including crop-spraying.

By 2003 the original fleet of five Tu-134A/AKs, six An-24s and more than two dozen An-2 biplanes had shrunk to four Tu-134s and three An-24RVs. An-24RV RA-46619 (c/n 37308706) illustrated here on the daily flight to Moscow-Domodedovo in 2002, is not one of the original six but a former Gorizont Aircompany machine acquired in 2000. The tail logo is a stylised Cyrillic letter Ch (Ч) with a wing.

Chitaavia

Yuriy Kirsanov

Founded in 1991 as the successor of the East Siberian CAD/Chita UFD, Chitaavia was one of the major airlines east of the Urals, operating scheduled passenger and cargo services with nine An-24Bs, three Tu-154B/B-2s, five Tu-154Ms and two An-26Bs and performing aerial work with eight An-2s, two Mi-8Ts and four Mi-8MTV-1s. It was announced in April 1998 that Chitaavia and Baikal Airlines would merge as part of a three-year economic and social co-operation agreement between the Irkutsk and Chita Regions. However, Baikal Airlines succumbed to the 1998 crisis. Chitaavia was also hard hit but weathered the gale, although the greater part of the fleet had to be sold or retired. Two Tu-154B-2s and two 'Ms are now the only active aircraft, including Tu-154M RA-85766 (c/n 92A923) seen here departing Moscow-Domodedovo.

CNG-Transavia

Voronezh-based CNG Transavia [–/CGT] started operations in 1995 with an An-12BK and two Yak-40s, although one of these was later returned to the lessor and replaced by an An-12BP. Both An-12s were transferred to to a Sharjah-based subsidiary and registered in Equatorial Guinea in 2000. In 2002 the airline became a member of Makarios Group and adopted a new livery, augmenting the original Yak-40KD with three more Yak-40s.

Left: Yak-40KD RA-21506 (c/n 9840259) in old CNG Transavia colours parked at Zhukovskiy on 23rd September 1999. *Dmitriy Komissarov*

Left and above: Yak-40K RA-88278 (c/n 9722053), a former Elbrus-Avia machine, seen at Moscow/Vnukovo-1 on 6th May 2003 illustrates the new livery. The letters 'CNG' are carried in small type on the tail only; the inset shows the badge on the nose.
Dmitriy Komissarov

Continental Airways

The Moscow charter carrier Continental Airways Joint-Stock Company (*Kontinentahl'nyye avialinii*) [PC/PVV] operated two Il-76TDs, including RA-76498 (c/n 0023442218, f/n 3105). The aircraft was bought in 1996 from the defunct Moscow Airways and flew in basic Moscow Airways colours with Continental Airways titles. It was eventually sold to the Iranian cargo carrier Atlas Air as EP-ALC in 1998. *Yuriy Kirsanov*

Today Continental Airways' fleet consists of two IL-86s and two Tu-154Ms, including RA-85760 (ex EW-85760, c/n 92A942) purchased from Gomelavia in 1999. It is seen here after pushback at Moscow/Sheremet'yevo-2 on 11th June 1999; the Belorussian origins are clearly indicated by the blue tail and blue engine nacelles with white stripes (which, incidentally, make a sharp contrast with the faded cheatline). At this stage the aircraft was completely anonymous; it was not until 2003 that it acquired Continental Airways titles (on the port side only) and tail logo. *Dmitriy Komissarov*

Dalavia Far East Airways

IL-62M RA-86131 (c/n 4255244) lines up on runway 32L at Moscow-Domodedovo for the daily flight to Khabarovsk. Manufactured in December 1992, this aircraft is one of the last IL-62Ms off the line. The titles on the port side are in Russian (Dal'avia Dal'nevostochnyye avialinii – Khabarovsk); the titles on the other side read 'Dalavia Far East Airways – Khabarovsk'. Incidentally, the Dalavia titles and logo did not appear until 1998; as late as November 1998 part of the fleet still flew in full Aeroflot colours. *Yuriy Kirsanov*

Dalavia Far East Airways, alias *Dal'nevostochnyye avialinii* [H8/KHB], is the post-Soviet identity of the Far Eastern CAD/1st Khabarovsk United Air Detachment established back in 1953. This large and important entity based at Khabarovsk-Novyy and comprising the 198th, 202nd and 289th Flights (operating the Tu-154, IL-62 and An-24/An-26 respectively) provided passenger and cargo services both along the Soviet Union's (Russia's) eastern coasts and to other regions westwards all the way to the capital.

Dalavia performs both domestic and international scheduled flights (notably to Japan). In early June 1999 the carrier signed a strategic co-operation agreement with Aeroflot enabling it to use the Russian flag carrier's offices abroad for passenger handling and aircraft maintenance.

As of now, the large fleet consists of ten An-24Bs, seven An-24RVs, seven An-26s, two An-26Bs, six Tu-154B-1s, six Tu-154B-2s, two Tu-154Ms, ten IL-62Ms and three Tu-214s. Dalavia was the launch customer for the latter type, taking delivery of the first production aircraft in May 2001. The two An-26ASLK navaids calibration aircraft have apparently been sold.

41

Looking rather weather-stained, Tu-154B-2 RA-85220 (c/n 77A220) awaits the next flight at Khabarovsk-Novyy in February 2002 in company with four sister ships. Interestingly, the nose titles still read 'Tu-154B'. Like some other post-Soviet air carriers, Dalavia has decided to 'leave well enough alone' (though it is arguable whether it is 'well'!) and made minimum changes to the 1973-standard Aeroflot livery. *Dmitriy Petrochenko*

Gleaming with fresh paint, Tu-214 RA-64503 (c/n 43103003) is pushed back to its allotted parking spot by a BelAZ-7420 airport tug within minutes after arrival from Khabarovsk on 17th August 2002. The airline's first Tu-214 is named *Yuriy Vorob'yov* in memory of the Tu-214's chief project engineer who died in July 2002. *Dmitriy Komissarov*

An-24RV RA-46522 (c/n 47310001), a very late-production example, taxies out at Khabarovsk-Novyy in 2002. Somewhat surprisingly, this aircraft wears the normal blue/white version of Aeroflot's basic livery rather than the red/white 'Polar' colours typical of Aeroflot aircraft operated in the High North and Far East. *Dmitriy Petrochenko*

Until 2003 Dalavia operated two An-26ASLK navaids calibration aircraft to support the operation of airports in the Russian Far East. RA-26571 (c/n 67303909) painted in basic Aeroflot Polar colours was one (it was later sold to Spetsavia); the other aircraft was RA-26673 (c/n 97308408). The characteristic fairing for the additional light on the port side is not visible in this view but the equally characteristic 'devil's pitchfork' aerials under the radome and the tailcone are, as are the four flush antennas built into the fin on each side instead of the usual two or three. *Dmitriy Petrochenko*

Daghestan Airlines

Daghestan Airlines (Avialinii Daghestana) [–/DAG] based at Makhachkala-Uitash is the successor of the North Caucasian CAD/Makhachkala UAD. The airline's initial fleet consisted of two Tu-154Ms, six An-24s, 13 An-2s used for agricultural and utility work and four Mi-8Ts. During the 1990s the Tu-154 fleet was doubled and the elderly An-2s disposed of.

Currently the fleet comprises three Tu-154Ms (the fourth aircraft, RA-85728, has been sold to Alrosa), two An-24s, one Mi-8T, one Mi-8MTV-1 (RA-25760) outfitted as a flying ambulance and two Tu-134B-3s acquired in September 2001 which are the most recent addition to the fleet. The airline performs scheduled domestic services, Moscow being the most important destination.

Pictured at Moscow/Vnukovo-1 in the summer of 2002, Tu-154M RA-85756 (c/n 92A938) was operated in the colours of former lessee Konveyer/Touch & Go (see page 148) for several years, finally gaining the Daghestan Airlines livery in 2003. The green, blue and red tail colours are those of the Daghestani national flag. RA-85840 is painted identically, while RA-85828 has a slightly different tail logo with a larger eagle (see next page). Note the small Cyrillic Avialinii Daghestana titles on the nose. The objects in the background are not remains of scrapped Vnukovo Airlines aircraft but workmen's huts. *Mike Kell*

Tu-154M RA-85828 (c/n 97A1009) seen starting up its engines at Moscow-Domodedovo on 4th October 2000 illustrates the earlier version of the tail logo with a white eagle. *Dmitriy Komissarov*

Tu-134B-3 RA-65569 awaits the next load of passengers to Makhachkala at Moscow/Vnukovo-1 on 6th May 2003. The livery of ex-owner Aviaexpresscruise (see page 29) was suitably amended by the addition of a Daghestan Airlines cheatline and tail colours. The other Tu-134B-3, RA-65579 (ex Sukhumi Airlines 4L-AAD, ex YL-LBF, ex CCCP-65696, c/n (03)63295, f/n 5802) is painted similarly but has a lighter shade of blue. *Dmitriy Komissarov*

Dobrolyot

Moscow-based Dobrolyot Airlines [–/DOB] were established in 1992 as the flying division of the NSA Soyuz aerospace industry company, inheriting the name of Aeroflot's precursor, a passenger carrier which ceased operations in 1922. The modern namesake is a cargo airline flying international and domestic charters. Launching operations from Moscow/Sheremet'yevo-1 and Zhukovskiy with a single An-12B and three former Soviet Air Force IL-76s *sans suffixe* built in 1974 and 1977 (the latter aircraft have now been retired, the airline later moved to Moscow-Domodedovo and still later to Moscow/Vnukovo-1, operating three IL-76TDs, two of which have been bought from the defunct Tupolev-Aerotrans (the Tupolev Design Bureau's house airline) and the third leased from Atran.

Demilitarised and somewhat anonymous IL-76 *sans suffixe* RA-76418 (ex CCCP-86640, c/n 073409237, f/n 0610) takes off from runway 07R at Moscow-Sheremet'yevo in 2000, showing the late version of the original tail logo. The Dobrolyot titles were painted out in connection with a lease to the British Overseas Development Agency in the mid-1990s and never restored. *Yuriy Kirsanov*

IL-76TD RA76389 (c/n 1013407212, f/n 8103) is unloaded at Moscow/Vnukovo-1 on 18th June 2002. The brown/white colour scheme is the basic livery of the aircraft's first civil operator, Arkhangel'sk-based Polis-Air. The aircraft is a former IL-76MD 'Falsie' (built with no tail gunner's station), having originally served with the Soviet/Russian Air Force as CCCP/RA-78852. This is revealed by the small elongated covers just ahead of the cargo ramp enclosing connectors for APP-50 strap-on chaff/flare dispensers and by the nose titles which have been changed from 'ИЛ-76МД' to 'ИЛ-76ТД' (note the last two letters applied over a darker patch of fresher paint). *Dmitriy Komissarov*

IL-76TD RA-76809 (c/n 1013408252, f/n 8203) awaits the next flight at Moscow/Vnukovo-1 on 6th May 2003. Like RA-76388 and RA-76389, this aircraft (which had been leased from Atran) sports the current version of Dobrolyot's titles and logo. *Dmitriy Komissarov*

Domodedovo Airlines

Established on 1st October 1960 as the Domodedovo as the Domodedovo UAD and known since 1st January 1979 as the Domodedovo Civil Aviation Production Association of the Moscow Territorial CAD (*Domodedovskoye proizvodstvennoye obyedineniye grazhdahnskoy aviahtsii*) comprising the 206th, 211th, 212th and 247th Flights, this is another major carrier serving the strategically important Far Eastern cross-country route. The carrier is notable for, firstly, having an all-Ilyushin fleet (until very recently) and, secondly, being one of the last Russian air carriers to operate the IL-18 turboprop as a passenger aircraft (the last two examples, RA-74267 and RA-74268, were sold in 1999).

On 12th January 1998 the Domodedovo CAPA [E3/DMO] reincorporated as Domodedovo Airlines Ltd. (*Domodedovskiye avialinii*) after a major reorganisation, but it was not until April 1999 that the appropriate Russian/English titles started appearing on the aircraft.

The good old IL-62M continues to form the backbone of the airline's fleet, 16 of the original 41 examples remaining on strength, although many are high-time airframes which will have to be retired soon, requiring replacement. There are also three IL-96-300s (Domodedovo Airlines is one of four operators of the type) and four IL-76TDs, although the freighters are perpetually leased to other carriers. In a surprise move,

Domodedovo Airlines acquired two ex-Lithuanian Airlines Yak-42D trijets (RA-42355 and RA-42359) in November 2002, although the former aircraft has been disposed of now.

Domodedovo Airlines operate scheduled flights to destinations within the CIS, trunk routes to Siberia and international charters to Europe, China, Malaysia, Singapore and, more recently, Egypt. The carrier consistently ranks among the Russian airline industry's leaders. Recently the carrier has been the subject of much controversy – unsurprisingly, since the competitors (such as Sibir') are less than happy to see Domodedovo Airlines expand its route network into their home ground.

Sporting the old 'Domodedovo Civil Aviation Production Association' titles and the DMO logo derived from the airline's ICAO designator, IL-62M RA-86465 (c/n originally applied as 62501 but then changed to 4625315 under the new system, which basically means the same) is caught by the camera a second before touching down on runway 14L at Moscow-Domodedovo. It was not uncommon for IL-62 pilots to engage reverse thrust before the aircraft had touched down, as this view testifies. RA-86465 had been retired by 2003. *Yuriy Kirsanov*

Being one of the last IL-18Ds off the line (it was manufactured on 9th December 1968), RA-74268 (c/n 188011201) was thus one of last to remain in service at Domodedovo and thus one of only three which stayed around long enough to gain Domodedovo CAPA titles and logos. Before transfer to the Domodedovo CAPA/212th Flight it had seen service as one of the two IL-18DORR long-range ocean fishery reconnaissance aircraft. It is seen here sitting on a sunlit apron at Moscow-Domodedovo on 18th November 1998; the following month the aircraft was sold to Tyumen' Airlines. *Dmitriy Komissarov*

RA-96006 (c/n 74393201003) is the second production IL-96-300 and the first of the type delivered to the Domodedovo CAPA's 206th Flight (which also operates IL-62Ms, as does the 211th Flight). It is seen here parked at Moscow-Domodedovo on 3rd November 1998 with the original 'Domodedovo Civil Aviation Production Association' titles. This aircraft and RA-96009 were delivered with a Russian flag on the tail, which they still have, despite switching to Domodedovo Airlines/Domodedovskiye avialiniï titles in the meantime; in contrast, the third example delivered (RA-96013) features the DMO tail logo. *Dmitriy Komissarov*

IL-76TD RA-76806 (c/n 1003403121, f/n 7901) taxies in after landing on Moscow-Domodedovo's runway 14L, displaying Domode-dovo Civil Aviation Production Association titles. More often than not the carrier's IL-76s are operated by other airlines, and this one is no exception: in October 2002 it was on lease with Airstars. *Yuriy Kirsanov*

IL-62M RA-86552 (c/n 2052345), the second-youngest in the fleet (it was built in February 1990), displays the new Domodedovo Airlines titles at its home base on 15th August 2002. Unlike some other aircraft, it has English titles on both sides.

Dmitriy Komissarov

IL-76TD RA-76812 on short finals to Moscow-Domodedovo, showing off the newly-applied Domodedovo Airlines titles. These did not last long, as the aircraft was leased to East Line shortly afterwards and then to Airstars (see page 14).
Yuriy Kirsanov

East Line

The IL-76 was the first type operated by East Line and remains the mainstay of the airline's cargo operations. IL-76s are leased from far and wide and wear an overwhelming variety of colour schemes. This is IL-76T RA-76462 (c/n 0013432955, f/n 2409) leased from Baikal Airlines, pictured on the west side of Moscow-Domodedovo's apron on 21st November 1998; the aircraft retains basic Aeroflot colours with large East Line titles, as simple as that.
Dmitriy Komissarov

By 1998 East Line had adopted an eye-catching green/white livery which was applied to part of the fleet, including IL-76TD UK-76449 (c/n 1003403058, f/n 7705) leased from Uzbekistan Airways, seen here retracting its undercarriage as it takes off from runway 32L at Moscow-Domodedovo in 1999. The aircraft wears the green-tailed variety of the full colour scheme and is named *Shenyang* after one of the key destinations served by the airline. Interestingly, despite the Uzbek prefix (Russian regulations do not require aircraft leased from other CIS states to be reregistered), the aircraft wears a Russian flag on the tail; the position of the registration on the outer engine nacelles is also noteworthy. UK-76449 has now been returned to the lessor. *Yuriy Kirsanov*

IL-76TD UK 76805 (c/n 1003403109, f/n 7808) wore the basic colours of Uzbekistan Intercargo Service from which it was leased in July 1999. It has now also been returned and belongs to Uzbekistan Airways. *Yuriy Kirsanov*

Established on 27 November 1995 as East Line Air but known as East Line Airlines [P7/ESL] since 1997, the carrier is based at Moscow-Domodedovo. Originally it was a pure cargo airline, becoming one of Russia's leading air cargo carriers by the late 1990s with services to Belgium, China, Greece, India, Italy, South Korea, Pakistan, Turkey and the UAE. Passenger services were started in 1997, initially within Russia, and the airline moved aggressively into the charter market (Egypt, Turkey, Italy and Greece are the principal destinations). Scheduled passenger flights were added in 1999. Furthermore, East Line effectively owns Domodedovo airport, which has international status since 1997, and has recently finished a complete reconstruction of the passenger terminal to increase efficiency add passenger appeal, including the addition of boarding 'fingers'.

Until 1999 the airline had no aircraft of its own, the large and constantly shifting fleet consisting of aircraft leased as required (often in the owner's colours with East Line titles). The few own examples included three IL-62Ms, a Tu-134A 'Salon' executive jet and a Mi-8PS VIP helicopter. East Line intends to stick to Soviet/Russian-built aircraft; types operated include the An-12 and IL-76TD freighters and the Tu-154B-2/Tu-154M, Yak-42 and IL-86 airliners. As of May 2003 the fleet included eight IL-76TDs (six 'true' and two 'Falsies'), two IL-76Ts, two IL-86s, one Tu-154B-2, three Tu-154Ms and one Yak-42D.

IL-76TD RA-76403 (c/n 1023412414, f/n 8604) leased from Vladivostok Air demonstrates the white-tail version of the full livery on the cargo apron at Moscow-Domodedovo on 3rd November 1998. The aircraft is named *Igor' Bykov* in memory of East Line's flight operations director killed in 1997. *Dmitriy Komissarov*

The vintage An-12 turboprop was also operated by East Line, albeit on a much smaller scale. Here, An-12B RA-11766 (c/n 401605) built in military configuration with a tail gunner's station sits on a rain-drenched apron at Moscow-Domodedovo on 3rd November 1998, with white-painted An-12BP RA-11112 (c/n 01347907) just visible beyond. Both aircraft were leased from/jointly operated with Avial'. *Dmitriy Komissarov*

This Ukrainian-registered An-12BP built in unarmed commercial configuration, UR-LAI (c/n 8345505) was leased from Volare Aviation Enterprise not later than November 1999, wearing basic Volare colours (complete with tail logo) with small East Line titles. Note that the type is actually marked on the nose as An-12BP. Other Volare Aviation Enterprise examples operated by East Line were An-12BKs UR-BWM and UR-LIP and 'military' An-12BP UR-SVG. *Yuriy Kirsanov*

East Line's first passenger aircraft was this Yak-42D, RA-42417 (c/n 4520423219110, f/n 0915) leased from Astrakhan' Airlines in 1997 and named *Volgograd* after the first destination the airline carried passengers to. It is seen here on the east side of Moscow-Domodedovo's apron on 3rd November 1998; the aircraft has since been returned. Unfortunately the example operated now, RA-42326 leased from Saravia, wears an altogether drab colour scheme with a white top, grey undersides, large East Line titles and no logo. *Dmitriy Komissarov*

East Line leased both of Buryatia Airlines' two Tu-154Ms remaining in service as of 1998. Here, RA-85829 (ex LOT Polish Airlines SP-LCD, c/n 87A755) taxies at Moscow-Domodedovo in mid-1998, looking magnificent in the full green/white livery. Small Cyrillic 'Buryatskiye avialinii' subtitles had been added underneath the East Line titles by October 1998. Unfortunately this sight can be seen no more: since July 2001 RA-85829 is operated by Enkor in all-white colours. *Yuriy Kirsanov*

The other Tu-154M leased from Buryatia Airlines (RA-85827) retained the basic colours of the lessor (see page 37), trading the elaborate yellow 'BURYA-TIA' titles for East Line markings. Here it is seen resting between flights at Moscow-Domodedovo on 3rd November 1998. An identical fate befell this aircraft in July 2001. *Dmitriy Komissarov*

East Line also operated three Tu-154B-2s leased from AVL Arkhangel'sk Airlines, including RA-85551 (c/n 82A551) seen parked at Moscow-Domodedovo on 18th November 1998. *Dmitriy Komissarov*

One of AeroBratsk's two Tu-154Ms, RA-85689 (c/n 90A860), was leased in November 2001; conveniently, the owner's titles did not have to be removed because none were applied yet! Here the aircraft is seen taxiing towards runway 32L at Moscow-Domodedovo on 15th August 2002. *Dmitriy Komissarov*

The 350-seat IL-86 widebody quickly became an important part of East Line's aircraft fleet. Initially leased aircraft were used, of course; one of the first to be leased was UK 86053 (c/n 51483203020) in full 1993-standard Uzbekistan Airways colours (except for the titles and flag), seen here parked at Moscow-Domodedovo on 20th September 1998. *Dmitriy Komissarov*

One of the most recent examples to be added to the fleet was UN 86068 (c/n 51483204035) leased form Air Kazakstan in June 2001. It is seen here taxiing out for take-off from runway 32L at Moscow-Domodedovo in 2001; the unusually bold registration is noteworthy. Sometime between April and July 2002 the aircraft was reregistered RA-86144 for unknown reasons, under which registration it is still operated. Since the registration had not been used before, this led more than one spotter to believe RA-86144 was a aircraft reimported from China until the c/n was checked! Actually East Line does have an ex-Chinese IL-86 but this is RA-86142 (ex-China Xinjiang Airlines B-2016). *Yuriy Kirsanov*

IL-86 RA-86085 (c/n 51483206056) was leased from now-defunct Vnukovo Airlines in March 2001, retaining basic Vnukovo Airlines colours. It is seen here parked at Moscow/Vnukovo-1 on 5th September 2001 shortly after return from lease and shortly before the owner's demise. *Dmitriy Komissarov*

In early 2001 East Line purchased a single Tu-134A-3 (4L-65798, c/n (03)63179, c/n 5701) from Georgian International Airlines. Duly reregistered RA-65798, it originally wore East Line's standard green/white livery as illustrated by IL-76TD UK-76449 on page 48. In the autumn of 2002, however, the refurbished aircraft was outfitted as a Tu-134A-3 'Salon', receiving this non-standard paint job. *Dmitriy Petrochenko*

East Line's fleet includes a single helicopter which is one of the few aircraft owned (not leased) by the carrier. Seen here in the static display of the Civil Aviation 2002 airshow at Moscow-Domodedovo on 15th August 2002, Mi-8PS-7 RA-24282 (c/n 98734415) is actually a former Mi-8T utility chopper converted to a luxurious 7-seater by the St. Petersburg Aircraft Repair Co. (SPARC); it was bought in April 2000. Note the airstair door to port characteristic of the Mi-8PS-7, the Kontoor weather radar (an unusual feature for a Mi-8PS) and the 475-litre external auxiliary tanks above the cabin windows, both added in the course of conversion. *Dmitriy Komissarov*

Elbrus-Avia

Based in Nal'chik, the capital of Kabardino-Balkaria, and deriving its name from the close proximity of Mt. Elbrus, the enterprise is mostly concerned with aerial work. The fleet includes no fewer than 62 Mi-2s, three Mi-8Ts and three Mi-8MTV-1s; the latter are used, among other things, for search and rescue operations in the mountains. The fixed-wing element consisted of three Yak-40s, but two have now been sold. Elbrus-Avia also leases Yak-42Ds as required.

Top: Yak-40 RA-87436 (c/n 9431235) in standard Elbrus-Avia colours at Moscow/Vnukovo-1 on 18th February 2002. By June it had been sold to CNG-Transavia, leaving identically painted RA-87500 as the sole Yak-40 in the fleet; Yak-40K RA-88278 (which had basic Aeroflot colours) was apparently sold around the same time.

Above: Yak-42D RA-42371 (c/n 4520422914225, f/n 0910), a former Volga Airlines machine seen here at Moscow/Vnukovo-1 on 6th May 2003, displays a non-standard livery featuring a white tail with a blue logo; RA-42362 operated previously had the correct full colours, while RA-42343 had a blue tail but lacked the EA logo. *Both Dmitriy Komissarov*

Enkor

The former Urals CAD/Chelyabinsk UAD/ 124th Flight emerged in 1994 as the Chelyabinsk Air Enterprise (*Chelyabin-skoye aviapredpriyatiye*) [H6/CHB], or Chelal (Chelyabinsk Airlines). Based at Chelyabinsk-Balandino, the carrier performed passenger and cargo services with three Yak-40 feederliners, three Tu-134A-3s, six Tu-154B/B-1/B-2s, seven Yak-42Ds and a single

Tu-154B-1 RA-85183 (c/n 76A183) taxies at Moscow-Domodedovo, displaying the carrier's original livery – ie, basic Aeroflot colours with Chelal bird logo on the nose. It was retired in 1999. *Yuriy Kirsanov*

An-12BP. Three second-hand Tu-154Ms acquired from Belavia and Aeroflot were added to the fleet in 1996-97.

In 1997 Chelal formed a charter subsidiary called Enkor [5Z/ENK], initially operating a pair of Tu-154B-2s in the parent company's colours. Both airlines took little damage from the 1998 crisis, showing a growth in passenger numbers in 1999. In 2001, however, a reorganisation led the parent company to vanish, the entire fleet being transferred to Enkor which became a scheduled carrier and changed its codes to [H6/ENK]. The airline's current fleet consists of three Tu-134A-3s, seven Yak-42Ds, a single Tu-154B-2 and five Tu-154Ms; most of them are operated in ex Chelyabinsk Air Enterprise colours.

Pictured at Moscow-Domodedovo on 18th November 1998, Tu-154B-2 RA-85514 (c/n 81A514) was one of two to wear the new Chelyabinsk Air Enterprise livery. It was also the first aircraft to be operated by Enkor, with which it still serves. *Dmitriy Komissarov*

RA-85725 (ex EW-85725, c/n 92A907) is one of two ex-Belavia Tu-154Ms bought in 1996, combining basic Belavia colours with the Chelal nose logo. It is seen here at Moscow-Domodedovo on 25th November 1998. *Dmitriy Komissarov*

Tu-134A RA-65118 (c/n (83)60462, f/n 4607) was the last of the carrier's three examples to gain full Chelyabinsk Air Enterprise colours, retaining the old titles after the addition of Enkor nose titles. Here it is shown at Moscow-Domodedovo on 17th August 2002. *Dmitriy Komissarov*

Gazpromavia

The largest fixed-wing aircraft operated by Gazpromavia is the IL-76TD, of which four are on strength. The aircraft are periodically leased to other carriers; here RA-76402, one of the original two examples (c/n 1023413430, f/n 8608), is seen on short finals to Moscow-Domodedovo, sporting the badge of the Sukhoi Design Bureau aft of the entry door to signify it has been leased by Sukhoi Aircompany. Previously RA-76402 was leased to Atlant-Soyuz; the latter airline leased it again in late 2002. The aircraft is in 1998-standard livery; note the bilingual Gazpromavia titles and the elliptical 'GAZ' tail logo, one of several variations used.
Yuriy Kirsanov

As the name implies, Gazpromavia Ltd. [–/GZP] established in March 1995 is the flying division of the powerful Gazprom corporation which controls Russia's natural gas industry. Operations were started on 16 April 1996. The original purpose of this air enterprise was to support the exploration of new gas fields and maintain operation of existing ones. This required a large fleet of fixed- and rotary-wing aircraft ranging from light utility helicopters used for resupply operations, pipeline patrolling etc. to large freighters for lugging heavy drilling equipment and pipes. Additionally, Gazpromavia acquired several airliners – originally for carrying teams of workers to and from cities in the vicinity of the gas fields where the work proceeds in shifts. However, the airline soon began using these aircraft on scheduled and charter flights, carrying ordinary paying passengers. The airline operates from Moscow/Vnukovo-1 and Ostaf'yevo, a Russian Naval Aviation base just south of Moscow which now doubles as an airport.

In addition to ordering new aircraft, Gazpromavia has expanded its fleet by absorbing several formerly independent aviation enterprises in the same industry, such as Moscow-based Mostransgaz (see page 142) and Nadym Gazprom.

The airline is the largest Russian operator of the An-74 which is operated in a variety of versions. The large fleet includes four IL-76TDs, twelve assorted An-74s, two Tu-134AKs, four Tu-154Ms, three Yak-40Ks outfitted as biz-jets, six Yak-42Ds and two Dassault Falcon 900Bs. The rotary-wing component comprises nearly two dozen Kamov Ka-26s, eight Mi-2s, 24 Mi-8Ts, two Mi-8PS-9 executive helicopters and 14 Mi-8MTVs/Mi-8AMTs. As a future replacement for the former two types Gazpromavia is considering both the Ka-226 and the Kazan' Helicopters Ansat.

The An-74 is numerically the airline's most important fixed-wing type; versions operated are the An-74T-100, An-74TK-100, An-74TK-100S, An-74-200 and An-74D. Due to the type's excellent short-field performance Gazpromavia's An-74s are regularly contracted to support rally-raids, including the famous paris-Dakar rally. Here, An-74T-100 RA-74008 (c/n 365.720.95.900, f/n 1405) is seen at its home base of Ostaf'yevo in the summer of 2002, still wearing "TV2 FRET" and 'Paris-Dakar' stickers (it was used to carry the TV crews' equipment during the 2001 rally). This aircraft wears the official Gazprom logo (unofficially called *zazhigalka*, 'lighter') on the tail and An-74-T-100 (sic) nose titles. The high-rise apartment blocks of Moscow are visible in the background.
Mike Kell

An-74-200 RA-74036 (c/n 365.470.98.965; f/n 1806?) shows a slightly different colour scheme as compared to the aircraft on the previous page (among other things, the tail logo is different and the belly is grey, not pale blue). Note also that the titles on this aircraft are in Russian only. *Yuriy Kirsanov*

Taken over from Nadym Gazprom as a standard An-74 in 1998, RA-74005 (c/n 365.470.94.892; f/n 1310?) has been updated to An-74T-100 standard; note the airstair door and the additional emergency exit to port, neither of which are featured in the baseline version. By 2002 the aircraft was fitted out for flying ambulance duties and redesignated An-74T-100S (for *sanitarnyy* – medical). It is seen here in the static park at the Civil Aviation-2002 airshow at Moscow-Domodedovo. Note the red '*Vozdooshnaya skoraya pomoshch*' (Air ambulance) titles on the centre fuselage which were added on the second day of the show (15th August). *Dmitriy Komissarov*

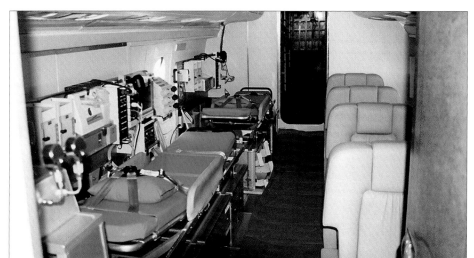

A look inside the rear cabin of An-74T-100S RA-74005, showing the stretchers and medical equipment on the starboard side, with seats for medical attendants to port. *Dmitriy Komissarov*

Seen here using reverse thrust after landing at Moscow-Vnukovo, Tu-154M RA-85774 (c/n 93A956) was acquired from Bashkirian Airlines in June 1998 and originally retained the basic 'hybrid' BAL colours, except for the titles and the tail logo. It was later repainted in Gazpromavia's current livery. *Yuriy Kirsanov*

Tu-134AK RA-65983 (c/n (03)63350, f/n 5808) is caught on short finals at Moscow-Vnukovo on 6th June 1999; the basic colours are those of Perm'transavia-PM, but 'Gazprom's Lighter' on the tail shows the ownership clearly. Note the truncated fairing under the APU jetpipe, a leftover from an HF aerial 'stinger' revealing the aircraft as a former Russian Air Force Tu-134 *Balkany* airborne command post (often misidentified as the 'Tu-135'). *Dmitriy Komissarov*

Gazpromavia's fleet includes six Yak-42D. RA-42438 (c/n 4520423609018) was delivered in November 1996 in this basic Aeroflot colour scheme with Gazpromavia titles in angular lettering and an early version of the tail logo (dubbed '*Gazprom v ogne*' – 'Gazprom on fire'). It is seen here at Ostaf'yevo in 2002. *RART*

Seen here in the static park at the Civil Aviation-2002 show at Moscow-Domodedovo, RA-42442 (c/n 4520422002019) is outfitted as a luxurious executive jet. It is the carrier's only Yak-42D to have this version of the full livery with the 'lighter' logo. *Dmitriy Komissarov*

Gazpromavia operates a large fleet of helicopters, the most important of which is the Mi-8. Most are 'first-generation' Mi-8Ts and Mi-8Ps, but anonymous-looking RA-25410 (c/n 96126) pictured at Ostaf'yevo is a Mi-8MTV-1 – or, more precisely, a Mi-172 heliliner/executive version featuring Mi-8P-style rectangular cabin windows, small rear clamshell doors-cum-airstairs and a forward airstair door. *RART*

Gromov Air

In 1992 the Flight Research Institute named after Mikhail M. Gromov (LII – *Lyotno-issledovatel'skiy institoot*) in Zhukovskiy formed its first commercial division, Volare Air Transport Co. [OP/VLR], for performing support operations (carrying delegations etc.) and flying business charters. In 1997 Volare was dissolved and replaced by a new airline, Gromov Air [–/LII, later –/GAI]. The current fleet comprises two Tu-134AKs, three Tu-134A 'Salons', a single Yak-40 'Salon 2nd Class' and four An-12 freighters. The airline flies business and cargo charters from Zhukovskiy and Moscow-Vnukovo, although in 2002 it briefly operated tourist charters with a Tu-154B-2 leased from Kavminvodyavia. Also, Gromov Air crews operate a Tu-134A-3M executive jet belonging to a private owner. The two IL-76s operated in the late 1990s have been disposed of.

Tu-134AK RA-65926 (c/n (33)66101, f/n 6336) parked at Zhukovskiy in August illustrates Gromov Air's old livery – actually slightly modified Volare colours. Note LII's badge on the nose. *Dmitriy Komissarov*

Resplendent in Gromov Air's latest livery, Tu-134A-3 'Salon' RA-65932 is seen at Moscow/Vnu-kovo-1 on 6th May 2003. Note the small English 'Gromov Air' titles on the cheatline and the Sukhoi OKB badge ahead of the entry door; the Sukhoi OKB owns this aircraft. *Dmitriy Komissarov*

All-white An-12BP RA-11650 (c/n 6344305) comes in to land, showing LII's stylised aeroplane logo on the nose. This aircraft (ex-Iraqi Airways YI-AES) was sold to Almaty Aviation in December 2002, becoming UN 11650. *Yuriy Kirsanov*

Ilavia

Ilavia [–/ILV], the Ilyushin Design Bureau's 'house airline' established in 1994 and based at Zhukovskiy, operated strictly Ilyushin aircraft, of course. (Yak-40 RA-88294 sometimes reported for Ilavia is actually operated by ILAN-L – see page 131.) The main type operated by the airline is the IL-76TD. Some of these aircraft are converted IL-76MDs leased from Transaviaexport. RA-76578 (formerly UR-76578 of Atlant-SV, c/n 0043449468, f/n 3707) is unusual, being its only demilitarised IL-76TD 'Falsie'; the radome of the PRS-4 Krypton gun-laying radar is clearly visible below the rudder, above the painted-over windows of the tail gunner's station. *Yuriy Kirsanov*

An aircraft that is no longer around. IL-76T RA-76521 (c/n 0003423699, f/n 1805), seen here beginning its take-off run on Zhukovskiy's runway 12, was bought from Abakan-Avia in early 1999; note that the titles are in Russian to port and in English to starboard. At the end of the year RA-76521 was sold to the Moldovan airline Aerocom, becoming ER-IBV.

Apart from IL-76s, Ilavia also operated two IL-18Vs (RA-75811 and RA-75834) in 1996-99. *Yefim Gordon*

Insat-Aero

Little is known about Insat-Aero, except that it is a business charter operator based at Moscow-Vnukovo and operating three jets leased from other carriers. This is Yak-40 'Salon 1st Class' (ex CCCP-87216, ex CSA Czech Airlines OK-FEI, c/n 9510440) seen at Moscow/Vnukovo-1 on 29th May 2000; it was previously operated by Air Vita and Aviaenergo as a Yak-40 'Salon 2nd Class'. Insat-Aero's other Yak-40 'Salon 2nd Class', RA-88276, is leased from the Bryansk Air Enterprise. *Dmitriy Komissarov*

Pictured here at Moscow/Vnukovo-1 in mid-2002, Tu-134B-3 'Salon' RA-65692 (a refitted aircraft with no rear door; c/n (03)63215, f/n 5705) was leased from ShaNS-Air in late 2000. RA-65692 had flown with SkyField in 1997-99 and previously belonged to LatCharter of Riga as YL-LBB until November 1996. *Mike Kell*

Izhavia

For ten long years Izhavia's four Tu-134A-3s wore Aeroflot colours without titles, as exemplified by RA-65056 (c/n (73)49860, f/n 3908) parked at Moscow-Domodedovo on 18th November 1998. *Dmitriy Komissarov*

The same aircraft at Moscow-Domodedovo on 15th August 2002, displaying the restrained but neverthe-less attractive new livery introduced in March 2002. RA-65141 followed suit in 2003. RA-65002 and RA-65842 ran out of service life before they had a chance to get a new livery. *Dmitriy Komissarov*

Yak-42D RA-42450 (c/n 4520424601019) is the newest aircraft in Izhavia's fleet, having been manu-factured in November 1996 and delivered in 1997. Like the two Tu-134A-3s remaining in service as of this writing, it carries 'Udmurtiya' titles, though nei-ther aircraft is a VIP jet operated for the republican government. *Yuriy Kirsanov*

Izhavia [–/IZA] was formed in 1992 as the successor of the Urals CAD/Izhevsk United Air Detachment, operating three An-2s, four An-24Bs, three An-26s, four Tu-134A-3s and a single Yak-42D. As the national airline of the Republic of Udmurtia, Izhavia flies domestic scheduled and charter services. As of now, two An-24s, two An-26s, two Tu-134As and the Yakovlev trijet remain operational, the other aircraft having been retired as time-expired.

Kaliningrad-Avia

Kaliningrad-Avia [K8/KLN] is the present identity of the Belorussian CAD's Kalinigrad UFD/312th Flight. (Sure, the Kaliningrad Region is part of Russia, but, being geographically separated from the Russian 'mainland', the region was also too small to form a separate CAD.) The fleet comprises eight Tu-134A-3s (out of an original ten) and two Tu-154Ms. For a while the airline operated foreign services jointly with Aeroflot. Hence aircraft in full Kaliningrad-Avia colours still carry small 'Aeroflot Russian International Airlines' titles aft of the flight deck, as illustrated here by Tu-134A-3 RA-65087 (c/n (73)60155, f/n 4306) arriving at Moscow-Domodedovo on the daily flight. *Yuriy Kirsanov*

KAPO-Avia

KAPO-Avia [–/KAO] is the flying division of the Kazan' Aircraft Production Association named after Sergey P. Gorboonov (*Kazahnskoye aviatsionnoye proizvodstvennoye obyedineniye*). From its base at Kazan'-Borisogleb-skoye it flies cargo and passenger charters with three IL-62Ms, an An-12BK, an An-26, a Tu-214 and a Yak-40. The single IL-76T 'Falsie' has been sold.

KAPO-Avia's aircraft wear a variety of liveries. RA-86586, the one-off IL-62MU combi aircraft with a reinforced floor (c/n 3357947), sports a blue cheatline and a larger tail logo. It is seen here on short finals to Moscow-Vnukovo's runway 24 on 17th March 2002. *Dmitriy Komissarov*

IL-62M RA-86945 (ex Czech Government Flight OK-BYV, c/n 3850145) is the latest addition to KAPO-Avia's fleet, becoming operational in April 2002. Originally it carried no tail logo and the registration was applied in larger characters. Ex-Orient Avia RA-86126 is painted identically. *Yuriy Kirsanov*

Resplendent in full company livery, An-26B RA-26597 (c/n 13310) sits at Zhukovskiy on 19th August 2003, the official opening day of the MAKS-2003 airshow, after bringing a KAPO delegation and the company's exhibits to the show. An-12BK RA-13392 wears the same colour scheme; the IL-62MU shown on the previous page originally had a blue tail, too. *Dmitriy Komissarov*

Karat

Over the years Karat has operated several An-24RVs. The first ones had a blue Aeroflot cheatline and Cyrillic titles on both sides; others, like RA-47264 (c/n 27307806) seen on 18th June 2002 during one of its frequent visits to Moscow/ Vnukovo-1, have all-white colours and English titles to port.
Dmitriy Komissarov

An-24RV RA-47361 (c/n 67310705) was leased from the Vladimir Air Enterprise and hence wore the striking orange/grey/white basic livery of the Avialeso'okhrana aerial forestry protection agency. Note the Cyrillic titles. *Yuriy Kirsanov*

Established in 1993 and originally doing business as Rikor Airlines, the Karat Joint-Stock Co. [2U/AKT, later V2/AKT] based at Moscow-Vnukovo operates scheduled and charter services in the CIS and abroad. The fleet consists mainly of aircraft leased from other airlines as required in a variety of colour schemes (for instance, the three Tu-134As leased from Astrakhan' Airlines in 1999-2001 did not wear Karat insignia at all). The current fleet comprises two An-24RVs, two Tu-134A-3s, one Tu-134AK, one Tu-134A-3M, one Tu-154B-2, one Yak-40K (outfitted as a Yak-40 'Salon 2nd Class' and operated for the Yava Tobacco Co.) and three ex-Latvian Yak-42Ds. The latter were leased from Kazan'-based Tulpar (see page 117); in 2003 Karat, which already had an alliance with the latter airline, initiated a merger with it.

The Yak-42 is the principal type operated by Karat. The first examples (for instance, RA-42427 leased from the Lipetk Air Enterprise) were again in basic Aeroflot colours; most, like RA-42528 (c/n 11041003) leased from the Ul'yanovsk Higher Flying School, are in all-white colours or have a grey belly. *Yuriy Kirsanov*

Radar-nosed Tu-134AK RA-65613 (ex CCCP-65613 No. 2, ex Interflug D-AOBD, ex DDR-SCO, c/n 3352106) was Karat's first Tu-134; it was bought from Komiinteravia in May 1999 and retained the basic colours of Yamal Airlines which previously leased it. The aircraft was sold to Alania in September 2000. *Yuriy Kirsanov*

Pictured here at Moscow/Vnukovo-1 on 6th May 2003, Tu-134A-3 RA-65137 (c/n (83)60890, f/n 4901) leased from the Kirov Air Enterprise was the first example to be painted in full white colours in February 2001. *Dmitriy Komissarov*

Three Tu-154B-2s are known to have flown in Karat colours, the first two (RA-85412 and RA-85468) retaining the Aeroflot cheatline. The third aircraft, RA-86358 (c/n 79A358) leased from the Kazan'-based airline Iron Dragonfly wears full colours with Russian titles to port and English titles to starboard. It is seen here at Moscow/Vnukovo-1 on 5th September 2001. The aircraft was named *S'uyumbiké* after the last empress of the Kazan' Khanate who was defeated by Czar Ivan IV the Terrible (note the blue ellipse near the forward entry door with the inscription *Сююмбикэ*); however, the name had been removed by 18th February 2002. *Dmitriy Komissarov*

One of two Yak-40s operated by Karat (and the only one to display Karat insignia visibly) was Yak-40 'Salon 2nd Class' RA-98113 (c/n 9710253) seen here at Moscow/Vnukovo-1 same day. The non-standard registration in the 981xx block reveals that the aircraft originally belonged to one of the divisions of the Ministry of Aircraft Industry. RA-98113 was leased or bought from Tulpar; the red cheatline is a leftover from previous ownership by another Tatar airline, Airstan. The aircraft wore only the Karat tail logo but no titles. *Dmitriy Komissarov*

Kavminvodyavia

Kavminvodyavia [KV/MVD], alias KMV (*Kavkazskiye Mineral'nyye Vody* – Caucasian Mineral Waters) is the former North Caucasian CAD/Mineral'nyye Vody Civil Aviation Production Association/209th Flight) based in Mineral'nyye Vody, a popular health resort. KMV has scheduled flights to over 50 Russian/CIS destinations. Charter flights are also operated regularly to Aleppo, Athens, Istanbul, Larnaca, Sharjah, Tel Aviv, and Thessaloniki all year round, and to Antalya, Malta and Varna in the summer season. The fleet comprises five Tu-134A-3s, one Tu-154B, nine Tu-154B-2s, three Tu-154Ms and two Tu-204-100s.

The Tu-154B-2 is the main aircraft type operated by Kavminvodyavia. The first two aircraft to receive the airline's smart livery – RA-85393 (c/n 80A393), seen here on short finals to runway 24 at Moscow-Vnukovo in September 1998, and RA-85457 – feature black KMV titles. *Dmitriy Komissarov*

Most Kavminvodyavia Tu-154B-2s, however, have more eye-catching red KMV titles, as exemplified by RA-85382 (c/n 79A382) at Moscow/Vnukovo-1 on 18th June 2002. Note how the service door ahead of the wings and the foremost emergency exit are outlined right over the titles. *Dmitriy Komissarov*

Kavminvodyavia also has three Tu-154Ms which are frequently leased to Iranian carriers. RA-85715 (c/n 91A891) is the oldest of the three; it is seen here shortly after disgorging passengers at Moscow-Domodedovo on 17th August 2002. This aircraft had flown with Iran Air Tours in 1998-99 as EP-MAX, among other things. *Dmitriy Komissarov*

RA-65139 (c/n (83)60915, f/n 4903) was the second Tu-134A-3 to be painted in full Kavminvodyavia colours and the first to receive red KMV titles. Here it is pictured during a turnaround at Moscow/Vnukovo-1 on 29th May 2000. RA-65126 originally had black KMV titles but was similarly repainted in 2001. *Dmitriy Komissarov*

RA-64022 (c/n 1450742064022 – not 1450743164022 as often reported) was the airline's second Tu-204-100 and the first example delivered new. Unlike other Russian operators of the type which had constant trouble with the aircraft's PS-90 turbofans at the start of the type's career, KMV enjoyed trouble-free operation. *Yuriy Kirsanov*

Kolavia

Kogalymavia Joint-Stock Co. (doing business as Kolavia) [7K/KGL] is the third-largest airline in the Tyumen' Region, with bases in Kogalym and Surgut. Established in May 1993, Kolavia operates scheduled passenger services to Moscow, Krasnodar, Nizhnevartovsk, St Petersburg, Rostov-na-Donu, Surgut, Ufa, Volgograd and Baku, as well as services and utility work within the region and domestic and international charters for oil companies. The current fleet comprises nine Tu-134A/AKs (mostly leased from other carriers), two Tu-154B-2s and five Tu-154Ms, plus six Mi-8T utility helicopters and three 'second-generation' Mi-8MTV-1s/Mi-8AMTs. Most of the Tu-154s bear the names *Kogalym* and *Surgut* after the airline's main bases.

Tu-154M RA-85784 (c/n 93A968) 'burns rubber' as it touches down on runway 32L at Moscow-Domodedovo in late 1996; the aircraft wears a small Kolavia logo on the nose. *Yuriy Kirsanov*

Tu-154M RA-85801 (c/n 93A960) taxies out for take-off from Domodedovo's runway 32R on 25th November 1998, showing off full Kolavia colours but no name. This aircraft was sold to Omskavia in February 2000. *Dmitriy Komissarov*

Seen at Domodedovo on 15th August 2002, radar-nosed Tu-134A 'Salon' RA-65943 is ex-Malév HA-LBR (c/n (13)63580, f/n 6102). The aircraft was outfitted with a VIP interior by Diamonite in May 2001. *Dmitriy Komissarov*

Komiinteravia

Tu-134A-3 RA-65902 (c/n (13)63742, f/n 6204) in an interim colour scheme (basic ex-Komiavia colours less titles/logo and with small Komiinteravia titles on the nose. *Yuriy Kirsanov*

Syktyvkar-based Komiinteravia [8J/KMV] was founded in 1996 as a branch of the huge Komiaviatrans (ex Komiavia, the successor of the Komi CAD established in 1992). The latter carrier was Russia's largest Tu-134 operator, with 42 of the type on strength, including 17 aircraft reimported from Germany. Operations were started in November on a small scale with two Tu-134AKs transferred from the parent company, joined in December 1997 by a Tu-134B. In September 1998, however, the Komi Regional Air Transport Directorate underwent a major reorganisation which resulted in tiny Komiinteravia taking over all of Komiaviatrans's heavy fixed-wing aircraft, leaving the latter carrier with a handful of An-2 and assorted helicopters.

Komiinteravia operates scheduled passenger flights from Syktyvkar to domestic destinations, as well as passenger and cargo charter flights to domestic and international destinations. The original fleet consisted of three An-12Bs (318th Flight), ten An-24B/RVs (366th Flight), 42 Tu-134A/AKs (75th Flight), three Yak-40s and six An-26s (based in Pechora). As of now, the freighters have been sold off, two Yak-40s, five An-24s and 20 Tu-134s remaining in service; many of the latter are leased to other carriers on a rotation basis.

Radar-nosed Tu-134AK RA 65609 of Komiavia (ex CCCP-65609 No. 2), seen here landing on Moscow-Vnukovo's runway 24 in 1994, retains the basic colours of Interflug with which it flew as D-AOBQ, ex DDR-SDG. Note the 'East German style' position of the registration and the Soviet flag on the rudder.

Tu-134AK RA-65977 (c/n (03)63425, f/n 5708) exemplifies Komiinteravia's current livery; the doors and emergency exits are not outlined. In Soviet days CCCP-65977 was operated by the Tashkent UAD/219th Flight as the the aircraft of Uzbek leader Karim Rashidov. *Both Yuriy Kirsanov*

Kosmos Airlines

Founded in 1994 as a division of the NPO Energiya aerospace industry corporation, Kosmos Airlines (originally Kosmos Aircompany [–/KSM] fly business and cargo charters from Moscow/Vnukovo-1 and -3 with three Tu-134AKs, a Tu-134A 'Salon', two An-12TBs and a single IL-76TD. Most of them wore a stylish livery with a red/white/blue cheatline and a blue tail with a Planet-Earth-cum-orbiting-satellite logo. The latest addition to the fleet, An-12BP RA-12957 (c/n 8345508) bought in 2001 as an attrition replacement, wears a partial Aeroflot 'polar' scheme with Kosmos tail colours and strange hybrid titles. It is seen here at Moscow/Vnukovo-1 on 5th September 2001.
Dmitriy Komissarov

Kras Air

Kras Air (Krasnoyarsk Airlines, or *Krasnoyarskiye avialinii*) is the successor of two air enterprises in the Krasnoyarsk CAD – the 1st Krasnoyarsk UAD (comprising the 128th, 214th and 400th Flights which operated the IL-62/IL-62M, IL-76T/TD and Tu-154 respectively) and the 2nd Krasnoyarsk UAD/126th Flight operating An-26s and Yak-40s. In 1993 it was privatised and organised as a joint-stock company. Over the years Kras Air has established a firm position as one of the heavyweights of the Russian airline market, operating scheduled regional passenger, international passenger, freight transportation, cargo handling and charter services in the CIS and abroad.

The passenger aircraft fleet includes two Tu-134As (the twinjets are leased as required), one Tu-154B-1, five Tu-154B-2s, 11 Tu-154Ms, three Tu-204-100s, two IL-62s, four IL-86s and one Yak-40. Cargo operations are handled by five IL-76Ts and three IL-76TDs. Fleet renewal is going slowly, the latest new aircraft (a Tu-204-100 named in memory of Aleksandr Lebed', the former governor of the Krasnoyarsk Region killed in a helicopter crash) being delivered in November 2003 – three years after the previous one. In 1995-97 Kras Air became one of the first Russian operators of Western aircraft, briefly leasing two DC-10-30s from McDonnell Douglas Corp. but returning them when operating them proved uneconomic. Yet today Kras Air is considering leasing Boeing 767-200s – both to add customer appeal and because Russian-built aircraft mostly do not comply with current noise and pollution regulations.

Kras Air is known for a huge variety of colour schemes. Initially many of the airline's aircraft were operated in basic Aeroflot colours with Kras Air titles, as illustrated by Tu-154B-1 RA-85201 (c/n 77A201) in 1998. *Yuriy Kirsanov*

Tu-154B-1 RA-85124 (c/n 75A124) sported unusual tail artwork with a blue 'arrow' (similar to the 'anti-soot' paintwork on Aeroflot's Tu-154Ms) and a stylised 'KA' (for Krasnoyarsk Airlines) in Russian flag colours. *Yuriy Kirsanov*

In 2000 Tu-154B-1 RA-85201 was leased to Sibaviatrans, also based in Krasnoyarsk. Here it is seen at Krasnoyarsk-Yemel'yanovo in 2002 after return from lease, still wearing basic Sibaviatrans colours with Kras Air titles and the latest version of the Kras Air logo. This veteran aircraft was still operational in February 2003. *Dmitriy Petrochenko*

Tu-154B-2 (c/n 81A505), seen here at Moscow-Domodedovo on 3rd November 1998, represents another variation on the theme, with Cyrillic 'Krasnoyarskavia' (КРАСНОЯРСКАВИА) titles in the break of the pinstripe below the cheatline and a blue outline version of the 'KA' badge (as seen on RA-85124) on the tail. *Dmitriy Komissarov*

Tu-154M RA-85702 (c/n 91A872) illustrates Kras Air's current livery. Note the small 'Krasnoyarskiye avialinii' (КРАСНОЯРСКИЕ АВИАЛИНИИ) subtitles.
S. and D. Komissarov collection

The fleet of the Krasnoyarsk CAD/1st Krasnoyarsk UAD/128th Flight included three re-imported from Poland, which were inherited by Kras Air. One of them, IL-62 RA-86709 (ex CCCP-86709, ex-LOT Polish Airlines SP-LAF, c/n 62204), is caught by the camera just as it is about to touch down on runway 14L at Moscow-Domodedovo, sweeping past Aviatrans Cargo Airlines' private apron visible beyond. *Yuriy Kirsanov*

Seen here at Krasnoyarsk-Yemel'yanovo in 2002, IL-62 RA-86453 (c/n 62202) remained operational long enough to receive Kras Air's current livery. This in one of the last active IL-62s *sans suffixe*. Note that the standard SPT-154 electrically propelled mobile gangway has been modified locally to feature a transparent roof over the steps.
Dmitriy Petrochenko

IL-86 RA-86121 (c/n 51483209089) sits parked at Moscow-Domodedovo on 18th October 1998 as Domodedovo Airlines IL-96-300 RA-96013 is pushed back in the background. This aircraft later became the first IL-86 to be repainted in Kras Air's current livery. *Dmitriy Komissarov*

An-26B RA-26139 (c/n 12901) on a snow-covered ramp at Krasnoyarsk-Yemel'yanovo in December 2002 after a heavy snowfall. *Dmitriy Petrochenko*

IL-76TD RA-76752 (c/n 0093498967, f/n 7502) flew in basic Aeroflot colours with Kras Air titles and small Aeroflot titles. On 5th April 1996 the crew of this aircraft intentionally departed from the approach pattern at Petropavlovsk-Kamchatskiy (Yelizovo airport) due to running low on fuel and the freighter crashed into Mt. Vashkazhech near Lake Nachikinskoye in poor weather, killing all on board. *Yuriy Kirsanov*

IL-76TD RA-76792 (c/n 0093497942, f/n 7406) was leased to Remex in 1997-99, retaining basic Remex colours after return from lease. This aircraft is equipped with BOZ-76 grids protecting the fuselage structure when bulk cargo is carried, a device developed by Kras Air's maintenance department . *Yuriy Kirsanov*

In July 1995 Kras Air leased former KLM Royal Dutch Airlines DC-10-30 N525MD (ex PH-DTA, c/n 46550, f/n 46) from the manufacturer. It was painted in McDonnell Douglas house colours, later gaining the Krasnoyarsk city crest on the fin. The aircraft was returned in 1997, going to Continental Airlines in October as N12089. The other DC-10-30 leased in April 1996 was N533MD (ex PH-DTD, c/n 46553, f/n 82, to Continental Airlines in August 1997 as N14090). *Yuriy Kirsanov*

In late 1999 Kras Air bought Tu-134A-3M RA-65930 (c/n (63)66500, f/n 6374), a former Tu-134SKh agricultural research aircraft converted into an executive jet – actually the first such conversion. The aircraft was sold to Karat in 2000. *S. and D. Komissarov collection*

Seen in the static park of the MAKS-2001 airshow, Tu-204-100 RA-64018 (c/n 1450741964018) is named after the Russian painter Vasiliy Soorikov. *Mike Kell*

Krylo

The airline Krylo [–/KRI] (*krylo* means 'wing' in Russian) based at Moscow-Bykovo and Zhukovskiy started operations in January 1991 with a single An-32 turboprop freighter (RA-48063). Later the carrier operated mainly IL-76s leased as required. Only one of them (RA-76379) actually belonged to the airline; like the abovementioned An-32, this aircraft looked rather anonymous, featuring a green cheatline and no titles. The current fleet consists of two IL-76TDs, both of which are converted from Belorussian Air Force IL-76MDs.

IL-76TD RA-78828 (ex-Transaviaexport EW-78828, c/n 1003401004, f/n 7601) wears basic Transaviaexport colours with Krylo titles and logo; the other example currently in service (EW-76710) is all-white with titles only. *Yuriy Kirsanov*

In 1999 Krylo briefly leased Mi-8PS RA-27189 (c/n 99357636) from an airline called Aero-Taxi in this star-spangled colour scheme. Actually this helicopter was built as a Mi-8T with circular windows and large clamshell cargo doors. On 28th September 1996 it crashed on Mt. Fisht near Sochi but was salvaged and rebuilt a Mi-8PS. Here it is seen in the static park of the MAKS-99 airshow. *Dmitriy Komissarov*

Kuban' Airlines

Kuban' Airlines Joint-Stock Co. (ALK – *Aviatsionnyye linii Kubani*) [GW/KIL] was formed in 1992 as the successor of the North Caucasian CAD/Krasnodar UAD which comprised the 241st, 336th and 406th Flights operating the An-24, Yak-42 and An-26 respectively. From its base at Krasnodar-Pashkovskiy airport the carrier operated scheduled flights in the CIS, as well as charters to Austria, Bulgaria, Cyprus, Germany, Greece, Egypt, Israel, Italy, Kuwait, Lebanon and the UAE. The current fleet comprises six Yak-42s, five Yak-42Ds and one An-24RV (out of an original 15), the 14 An-26s having been sold in 1997-99. Here, Yak-42 RA-42350 (c/n 4520424711372, f/n 0808) is seen on finals to runway 24 at Moscow-Vnukovo in September 1998. *Dmitriy Komissarov*

An-24RV RA-46668 (c/n 47309406) was one of very few to wear full Kuban' Airlines colours. The aircraft was no longer in the fleet as of this writing.
Yuriy Kirsanov

Lipetsk Avia

The Lipetsk Air Enterprise, lately known as Lipetsk Avia [–/LIP], is the new identity of the Central Regions CAD/Lipetsk United Air Detachment. The enterprise performs regional, scheduled and charter passenger services and some aerial work. The large fleet includes nine passenger- and VIP-configured Yak-40s, three Yak-40Ks and two Yak-42Ds operated by the former 275th Flight, as well as two dozen Mi-2 helicopters and 40 An-2 biplanes used for crop-spraying and other utility work. Many of the jets are leased out or operated for various industrial enterprises.

Seen here parked at Moscow/Vnukovo-1 on 6th May 2003, Yak-40 'Salon 2nd Class' RA-87845 (c/n 9331430) illustrates the simple livery of Lipetsk Avia. The break in the cheatline is made to resemble a Cyrillic L (Л). *Dmitriy Komissarov*

Though not originally a Yak-40 'Salon 2nd Class', as indicated by the lack of white 'plugs in the foremost cabin windows, RA-88236 (c/n 9640551) was outfitted with a VIP interior and received this striking colour scheme when it was leased by the Lipetsk-based Stinol company producing household refrigerators. Here the aircraft is towed to its assigned parking spot in the static display of the MAKS-99 airshow on 21st August 1999. Regrettably the aircraft had been repainted in a similar manner to RA-87845 by March 2001, except that the Stinol logo is carried on the tail in lieu of the Russian flag and no titles are applied. *Dmitriy Komissarov*

LUKoil Avia

LUKoil, one of the largest Russian oil companies, had long made use of three VIP-configured Yak-40s and a Yak-142. Originally these were operated by Avcom but eventually most of them were transferred to LUKoil Avia, the company's flying division based at Moscow/Sheremet'yevo-1. The current fleet consists of two Yak-40 'Salons 2nd Class', one Yak-142, two Hawker 700s (BAe 125-700s) and one Dassault Falcon 900EX; the Western biz-jets are registered in the Bermudas.

Yak-40 'Salon 2nd Class' RA-87353 (c/n 9330231) wears LUKoil's red/white house colours and the company logo on the tail. This aircraft was previously operated by Transaero Express.
Yuriy Kirsanov

Yak-40 'Salon 2nd Class' RA-88297 (c/n 9530142) was originally operated by the Soviet Air Force as '01 Red'. It wears a rather different colour scheme with a Kolavia tail logo and the LUKoil badge on the fuselage. *Yuriy Kirsanov*

RA-42424 was built in October 1992 as a Yak-42D with the c/n 4520424219141 (f/n 0216), serving as a Yakovlev OKB demonstrator. In 1995 it was converted to a Yak-142 for LUKoil, receiving the new c/n 4520421502016. *Yuriy Kirsanov*

Mavial Magadan Airlines

Seen here taking off at Moscow-Vnukovo, Tu-154M RA-85667 (c/n 89A825) displays Mavial Magadan Airlines' standard livery. *Yuriy Kirsanov*

Tu-154M RA-85677 (c/n 90A839) pictured taxiing out for take-off at Moscow/Sheremet'yevo-2 in 2002 has a non-standard colour scheme with an 'anti-soot' blue rear fuselage. The aircraft wears the Magadan city crest and '*Magadan shest'deyat let*' titles to mark the 60th anniversary of the city's foundation. *Dmitriy Petrochenko*

MAUS

'Mouse'...? No, the funny-sounding name has nothing to do with mice; it is an acronym for *Myachkovskiye aviausloogi* (Myachkovo Air Services). Transformed from a specialised flight of the Central Regions CAD/Myachkovo UAD, the company operates ten examples of the An-30 photo survey aircraft, some of which are in the An-30M 'sky cleaner' version. Most are still in Aeroflot colours, but RA-30035 (c/n 0702) wears appropriate *Myachkovskiye aviausloogi* titles. *Mike Kell*

Meridian Airlines

Built as a Tu-134SKh agricultural survey aircraft and operated by the Ivanovo State Air Enterprise in its latter days as such, RA-65725 (c/n (63)66472, f/n 6371) was sold in 2001 and converted to a Tu-134A-3M executive jet for the Sibur Holding Co. which owns several Russian car tyre factories. By February 2002 the aircraft had been resold to Meridian Air, gaining appropriate titles in small lettering on the forward fuselage but retaining the stylised S tail logo of the previous owner and this stylish green/grey/white colour scheme. *S. and D. Komissarov collection*

Business charter operator Meridian Air Joint-Stock Co. [–/MMM] started operations from Moscow/Vnukovo-1 in 1992 with a BAe 125-700 and a BAe 125-800 operated for Master Group. The latter jet was later sold but two Tu-134A-3M executive jets were added instead, one of which remains now.

The same aircraft at Moscow/Vnukovo-1 on 6th May 2003, now with the proper Meridian Air tail logo and a 'golden sun' logo aft of the entry door. Vnukovo Airlines IL-86 RA-86010, a dead aircraft belonging to a dead airline, is visible beyond. *Dmitriy Komissarov*

Bought from the Tupolev Joint-Stock Co. on 3rd March 2001, the Tu-134SKh prototype (CCCP-65917, c/n (33)63991, f/n 6329) was converted to a Tu-134A-3M and reregistered RA-65917. It received the same basic colour scheme but in a red/yellow/white version and with a 'golden sun' tail logo. It is seen here at Moscow/Vnukovo-1 on 6th May 2003. RA-65917 is identical to RA-65725 as regards the window arrangement (1+door+7+1+exit+2+1 to port and door+7+1+exit+2 to starboard) but retains the tall starboard strake aerial on the centre fuselage associated with the A-723 long-range radio navigation system. In December 2003 the aircraft was sold to an unidentified Ukrainian company, becoming UR-65917. *Dmitriy Komissarov*

Meridian Air's first aircraft, BAe 125-700B RA-02801 (ex G-BHTJ, ex G-5-810, c/n 257097) awaits the next mission at Moscow/Vnukovo-1 on 29th May 2000. This aircraft was originally operated for Magnitogorsktyazhprom (Magnitogorsk Heavy Industries) and later for the Patina & Charter Air Centre. *Dmitriy Komissarov*

Omskavia

Omskavia [N3/OMS] came into being on 1st February 1994 when the Omsk United Air Detachment of the former West Siberian CAD was organisationally separated from Omsk-Fyodorovka airport.

Omskavia is a public limited company with 51% of the stock owned by the employees, 20% by the state and 29% by other shareholders. It operates scheduled passenger services in the CIS and passenger charters abroad; cargo operations have been discontinued after the sale of the sole An-26. The airline also maintains its own and other organisations' aircraft and other aviation equipment.

The current fleet comprises two An-24s of the original four and ten Tu-154Ms, the six Tu-154B-1/B-2s having been sold or retired. Omskavia frequently leases its Tu-154Ms to Iranian charter carriers.

Until the mid-1990s Omskavia' fleet was operated in basic Aeroflot colours with Cyrillic Omskavia titles, as illustrated here by Tu-154M RA-85752 (c/n 92A934) at Moscow-Domodedovo on 3rd November 1998. Note the tell-tale exhaust stains on the rear fuselage aft of the engine nacelles caused by thrust reverser operation. This aircraft never received the full airline livery (currently it has a grey/white colour scheme with green Omskavia titles in English and no cheatline). *Dmitriy Komissarov*

Tu-154B-2 RA-85504 (c/n 81A504) was acquired from Severaero in early November 1998; it is seen here on 18th November at Moscow-Domodedovo with Omskavia titles but still wearing Severaero's leaping stag tail logo. The bright blue radome is an unusual feature. The aircraft had been sold by May 2000. *Dmitriy Komissarov*

Tu-154B-2 RA-85291 (c/n 78A291) illustrates Omskavia's first livery of its own devised in 1995; here the aircraft is shown in 1998 following an upgrade from its original Tu-154B-1 configuration. The tail logo represents green fir-trees, not a lightning bolt. Note that the titles are in English on this aircraft. In 1998 RA-85291 was sold to Chernomor-Avia. *Yuriy Kirsanov*

Tu-154M RA-85818 (c/n 85A719) was bought from Cubana, with which it flew as CU-T1276; originally it had been delivered to Guyana Airways as 8R-GGA. Here it is just about to touch down on runway 14L at Moscow-Domodedovo. This aircraft features Cyrillic Omskavia titles; interestingly, the 'Tupolev-154M' titles on the engine nacelles are applied in exactly the same lettering as on Balkan Bulgarian Airlines aircraft. *Yuriy Kirsanov*

Tu-154M RA-85730 (c/n 92A912) flew in basic Aeroflot colours until 2000, after which it received Omskavia's stylish current livery with twin cheatlines. Some aircraft, including Tu-154M RA-85714, feature a slightly different earlier version with an all-white fuselage. The jagged green 'fir tree' artwork on a red background on the tail has given rise to the nickname *Zmey Gorynych* (dragon in Russian folklore). *Yuriy Kirsanov*

Orenburg Airlines

Orenburg Airlines [R2/ORB] were formed in 1992 as the new identity of the Volga CAD/Orenburg UAD which was established in 1932. From its base at Orenburg-Tsentral'nyy airport the carrier operates scheduled domestic passenger services to 42 destinations and inclusive tour charters, including services to Frankfurt, Nürnberg and Genoa via Simferopol'. Orenburg Airlines was the first Russian domestic airline to introduce the hub system of connecting flights in Orenburg, providing a full for transfer passengers, and the first Russian domestic airline to introduce through air fares.

The current fleet includes five Tu-134A-3s, four Tu-154B-2s, a single Tu-154M, five An-24Bs and three Yak-40s. The airline also carries out aerial work with 36 An-2 utility biplanes and at least one Mi-8MTV-1.

Tu-134A-3 RA-65860 (c/n (53)28265, f/n 2805), is serviced on a snow-covered apron at Moscow-Domodedovo on 20th November 1998. This aircraft is now retired. *Dmitriy Komissarov*

RA-85768, Orenburg Airlines' sole Tu-154M (c/n 92A949), taxies out for take-off from Moscow-Domodedovo's runway 32R on 25th November 1998 in brilliant sunshine. The pale shade of blue used on the cheatline and rudder is noteworthy. *Dmitriy Komissarov*

Tu-154B-2 RA-85603 (c/n 84A603), one of four in the fleet, sits under threatening skies at Moscow-Domodedovo on 3rd November 1998. Like RA-65602 andRA-65604, it was originally a Tu-154B-2 'Salon' with special HF communications gear operated by the Soviet government flight. *Dmitriy Komissarov*

Perm Airlines

Tu-134A-3 RA-65064 (c/n (73)49886, f/n 4006) takes on a load of passengers and luggage at Moscow/Vnukovo-1 on 29th May 2000. Since then the airline has shifted its Moscow flights to Domodedovo. Most of the airline's Tu-134s looked like this all along; RA-65775 had an Aeroflot-style cheatline which was later painted out. *Dmitriy Komissarov*

Perm Airlines (**Perm**skiye avia**lin**ii) [UP/PGP, later 9D/PGP]is the successor of the Urals CAD/1st Perm' UAD based at Bol'shoye Savino airport. The airline operates scheduled domestic flights and domestic/international charter services; the latter include Baku, Yerevan, Tashkent, Tbilisi, Istanbul, Sharjah and Tenerife.

The current fleet consists of two An-24Bs, two An-26s, five Tu-134A-3s, two Tu-154B-1s, one Tu-154B-2 and a Yak-40. The two Tu-204-100s leased from the manufacturer in the mid-1990s (RA-64016 and RA-64017) have been returned, the planned purchase of a third Tu-204 thus automatically being cancelled.

Pictured after landing at Moscow-Domodedovo's runway 32L, Tu-154B-1 RA-85217 (c/n 77A217) was the oldest of the type in Perm Airlines' fleet. It never received the full livery and was retired in late 2002 looking as shown here. *Yuriy Kirsanov*

Perm Airlines was the first commercial operator of the fully certificated Tu-204-100. Here RA-64016 (c/n 1450743464016) is seen at Zhukovskiy in the static park of the MAKS-95 airshow shortly before delivery. Originally this aircraft had been earmarked for delivery to Aeroflot Russian International Airlines and then to Vnukovo Airlines. The leasing payments for the Tu-204s taxed Perm Airlines' resources too heavily, forcing the carrier to return both aircraft. *Sergey Komissarov*

Tu-154B-2 RA-85450 at Moscow-Domodedovo after return to Perm Airlines, wearing the proper full livery. *Dmitriy Petrochenko*

Polyot/Flight

Founded in 1989, Polyot (alias Flight) was originally known as Polyot Russian Airlines (*Rosseeyskaya aviakompaniya Polyot*) [–/POT] was founded in 1989, starting operations with two An-12BPs (RA-11320 and RA-11325) which were sold in 1998-99. In 1993 the airline moved into the passenger air transport market. Illustrated here is Yak-42D RA-42428 (c/n 4520422306016) was acquired in 1995. Strangely enough, it wore this old-style colour scheme as applied to the An-12s with a striped tail featuring a bird logo in a circle. *Yuriy Kirsanov*

In 1994 Polyot took delivery of its first An-124 Ruslan heavy transport, eventually increasing the fleet to eight An-124-100s. The An-124 introduced this livery with a blue belly and a blue tail with sloping stripes. Here, RA-82077 (c/n 9773054459151, f/n 07-09), the second example delivered, comes in to land at Moscow-Domodedovo. Note the airline's telephone/fax numbers and old-style logo applied to the underside of the grey-painted nose visor so that they become visible when the nose swings open for loading and unloading. At least one of the Ruslans (RA-82010) is slated for conversion to An-124VS configuration for air launch of small satellites. *Yuriy Kirsanov*

Polyot operates two Yak-40s. The second aircraft, RA-88304 (c/n 9510439) acquired in early 2003, is shown here at Moscow-Vnukovo's maintenance base on 6th May 2003. This is ex Centrafricain TL-ACP (ex-Air Pass 3D-YAK, ex-Estonian Air ES-AAR, ex-CCCP-87333), so logically it should have become RA-87333. The aircraft wears a non-standard livery with a white belly and blue/red/blue pinstripes
Dmitriy Komissarov

Yak-40 RA-87541 (c/n 9530642) bought in 1993 was Polyot's first airliner, also gaining full company livery.
Yuriy Kirsanov

Pskovavia

Pskovavia [–/PSW] is the new identity of the Leningrad CAD/Pskov UFD/320th Flight operating An-24 airliners and An-26 freighters from Kresty airport which is also a major Russian Air Force base. The airline flew domestic and international cargo charter services. The current fleet comprises six An-26Bs, the nine An-24B/RVs having been disposed of.

An-26B RA-26100 (c/n 27312304) undergoes routine maintenance at its home base in 2002. The aircraft was previously leased to Air Charter Service of Liberia and still carries the ACS logo on the tail.
Dmitriy Petrochenko

Dmitriy Komissarov

Primair

Based at Moscow-Domodedovo, Primair [–/PMM] started operations in 1999, flying passenger charters. The fixed-wing fleet of two Tu-134AKs and one Tu-134A has now been reduced to one aircraft; on the other hand, six Mi-2 utility helicopters have been added. Here, the sole remaining jet, Tu-134AK RA-65097 (c/n (83)60540, f/n 4704) is seen at Moscow-Domodedovo on 15th August 2002. The aircraft is operated for the Moscow City Department of Construction since 1999, bearing an appropriate badge on the port side near the forward entry door

Pulkovo Air Enterprise

Founded way back in 1932, the Leningrad CAD/1st Leningrad UAD comprising the 67th Flight (operating a mix of Tu-154s and An-12 freighters), the 205th Flight (flying Tu-154s and IL-86s) and the 344th Flight (operating Tu-134) became the St. Petersburg Air Enterprise, subsequently renamed Pulkovo Air Enterprise [Z8/PLK, later FV/PLK]. It was a state unitary aviation enterprise comprising the airline itself and

For years the Pulkovo Air Enterprise's aircraft wore Aeroflot colours, as exemplified by Tu-134A-3 RA-65128 (ex Lithuanian Airlines LY-ABI bought in March 1995, c/n (83)60628, f/n 4710) climbing away from runway 22R at Copenhagen-Kastrup in July 1998. *Dmitriy Komissarov*

It was not until 1997 that Pulkovo introduced its own livery as illustrated by Tu-154M RA-85695 (c/n 91A868), a former Baikal Airlines machine bought in 1999, coming in to land. Note the small Aeroflot titles under the rear entry door and the St. Petersburg city crest aft of the flight deck. *Yuriy Kirsanov*

St. Petersburg's international airport which gave the airline its name. After the 'demolition' of the old Aeroflot the Pulkovo Aviation Enterprise was one of the few to actively oppose the organizational separation of the airline and its home airport. This was no easy thing and the airline had to fight out its standpoint with government institutions and influential industry organizations which treated it with indifference, at best – or open hostility.

Apart from scheduled and charter domestic and international services (initially under Aeroflot's SU flight code), in 1999 Pulkovo provided passenger and cargo handling and catering services for 52 Russian and foreign scheduled carriers. The airline has alliances with El Al, LOT Polish Airlines, Sayakhat and SAS Scandinavian Airlines.

The current fleet comprises eleven Tu-134As, ten Tu-134B-2s, 15 Tu-154Ms and eight IL-86s (a ninth was lost in the type's first fatal crash in 2002); the seven aged An-12B freighters have been phased out. Currently the Pulkovo Air Enterprise is starting a fleet renewal programme and has placed an order for five Tu-334-100s.

Recently repainted Tu-134A-3 RA-65759 (ex Estonian Air ES-AAO bought in August 1995, c/n (93)62239, f/n 5110) sits parked at Moscow-Domodedovo on 17th August 2002. Most Pulkovo aircraft wearing full colours have this dark blue colour, only Tu-134A RA-65004 and Tu-154B-2 RA-85530 having a lighter shade. *Dmitriy Komissarov*

Tu-154B-2 RA-85346 (c/n 79A346) was one of an original 27 Tu-154B-1s and 'B-2s. It was retired before it could be repainted in Pulkovo's modern colours. *Yuriy Kirsanov*

Rodina

Rodina ('Motherland' in Russian) is a new airline established in 2002 and operating three former Kolpashevo Air Enterprise An-28 feederliners (RA-28927, RA-28929 and RA-28939) from Moscow-Myachkovo, performing VIP transportation and para-dropping.

RA-28939 (c/n 1AJ 009-05) depicted here at its home base, wears this flamboyant colour scheme. *Dmitriy Petrochenko*

Rossiya State Transport Co.

The IL-62M was the 235th Independent Air Detachment's (and, until recently, the Rossiya State Transport Company's) most important type, two IL-62M 'Salon TM-3SUR' VIP aircraft equipped with Surgut HF comms serving as the presidential jets. Here, one of the 'lower-ranking' IL-62M 'Salons' lacking HF comms gear (RA-86466, c/n 2749316) is shown in its original 1993-standard livery with small РОССИЯ (Rossiya) titles on the extreme nose. *Yuriy Kirsanov*

IL-62M RA-86712 (c/n 4648339) in the 1995-standard livery dubbed *gherbovaya raskrahska* ('coat-of-arms livery'). *Yuriy Kirsanov*

RA-86466 taxies at Moscow/Vnukovo-1 on 5th September 2001, showing the airline's current livery introduced in July 1997 (dubbed *seryy oozhas*, 'abominable grey'). *Dmitriy Komissarov*

On 3rd December 1993 the 235th Independent Air Detachment (the Soviet Federal Government flight) based at Moscow-Vnukovo became GTK Rossiya (*Gosoodarstvennaya trahnsportnaya kompaniya 'Rossiya'* – Russia State Transport Co.) [R4/SDM]. The enterprise provides mainly VIP flights on behalf of the Russian government, including operation of the presidential aircraft. Since you cannot make much of a living carrying government officials alone, in 1998 GTK Rossiya started flying passenger charters, later launching scheduled services to several destinations, including the Black Sea resorts of Sochi and Anapa. Hence a major portion of the airline's fleet has been delivered in (or converted to) tourist class configuration.

The IL-96-300PU presidential jet became the flagship of GTK Rossiya's fleet in 1995. The first of two, RA-96012 (c/n 74393201009), is seen here, showing the characteristic fat spine housing satellite comms/navigation antennas and three blade aerials ahead of it. *RART*

The second IL-86-300PU(M), RA-96016 (c/n 74393202010), nearing completion at the Voronezh aircraft factory in July 2002. Note the IL-86 style integral airstairs. *Dmitriy Petrochenko*

The Tu-154 is GTK Rossiya's main medium-range type. Here, Tu-154M RA-85653 (c/n 89A795) in 1993-standard livery. This aircraft was sold to the Vnukovo aircraft overhaul plant in 2001. *Yuriy Kirsanov*

Additionally, some aircraft are operated jointly with Aeroflot

The airline's fleet includes two elderly IL-18Ds used as communications relay aircraft, ten IL-62Ms, two IL-96-300PUs, eleven Tu-134AKs, seven Tu-154Ms, three Tu-214s and seven Yak-40s. Since the IL-96-300PU was introduced when Boris Yel'tsin was President, the PU is not a reference to Vladimir Putin but stands for *poonkt oopravleniya* (command post). The rotary-wing element comprises six 'first-generation' Mi-8PS-7/Mi-8PS-9s and two purpose-built presidential Mi-172 'Salons'.

Delivered in May 2001, Tu-154M RA-85843 (c/n 01A991) is the newest example in the fleet and has a 158-seat mixed-class layout. It is seen here at Moscow/Vnukovo-1 on 18th June 2002.
Dmitriy Komissarov

Prior to the formation of GTK Rossiya the Tu-134AKs of the Russian government flight, including RA-65912 (c/n (23)63985, f/n 6325) retained Aeroflot titles but had grey tails. *Yuriy Kirsanov*

Tu-134AK RA-65921 (c/n (33)63997, f/n 6334) in the 'abominable grey' livery is seen on short finals to Moscow-Vnukovo's runway 24 on 20th May 2000.
Dmitriy Komissarov

Yak-40 'Salon 1st Class' (note the white plugs in the first two windows) RA-65968 (c/n 9841258) in the days when it wore the 'coat-of-arms' colour scheme.
Yuriy Kirsanov

In spite of its VIP interior, Yak-40D RA-87970 (c/n 9831458) is jointly operated with Aeroflot. It is seen here in the current grey livery as it approaches Moscow-Vnukovo's runway 24 on 16th February 2002 on a scheduled flight from St.Petersburg. Another example, RA-87971, actually wears additional 'Aeroflot' titles beneath the windows.

Dmitriy Komissarov

In 1994-99 the Rossiya State Transport Co operated two An-124-100 Ruslan 'big lifters' for carrying government limousines and secure communications equipment during state visits. RA-82072 (c/n 9773053359136, f/n 07-05) is seen here taxiing in at Moscow-Vnukovo after a training flight in 1995. Both Ruslans were sold to Antonov Airlines in 1999, becoming UR-82072 and UR-82073. *Yuriy Kirsanov*

Ryazan'aviatrans

Ryazan'aviatrans [–/RYZ] was formed in 1992 as the successor of the Central Regions CAD/Ryazan' UAD, operating regional scheduled flights and performing aerial work from Ryazan'-Turlatovo. The current fleet consists of six Mi-2 helicopters and two An-24RVs, the five Let L-410UVP feederliners having been retired. Here, An-24RV RA-47362 (c/n 67310706) awaits the next flight at Moscow.Vnukovo-1 on 18th June 2002.

Dmitriy Komissarov

Saturn (ex Rybinskiye Motory)

The Rybinsk Engine Co. (Rybinskiye Motory) established in 1937 as a Ministry of Aircraft Industry operates a small fleet of two combi-configured Yak-40Ks and a single An-26 freighter from Ryybinsk-Starosel'ye. In 2002 Rybinskiye Motory [–/RMT] changed its name to Saturn, being closely associated with the Lyul'ka-Saturn aero engine design bureau. Here, Yak-40K RA-87225 (c/n 9841359) in the old Rybinskiye Motory livery disgorges a load of passengers after arriving at Moscow/Vnukovo-1 on 29th May 2000.

Dmitriy Komissarov

Sakha Avia

Sakha Avia [K7/IKT], the successor of the huge Yakutian CAD, is one of the biggest Russian air carriers, the national airline of the Republic of Yakutia (Sakha). It is headquartered in Yakutsk and comprises the Batagai, Chokurdakh, Kolyma-Indigirka, Magan', Neryungri, Nyurba, Tiksi, Ust'-Nera, Yakutsk and Zyryanka divisions. The airline has scheduled passenger and cargo services in the CIS and flies international cargo charters. Today, Sakha Avia is suffering from excessive capacity and much of the huge fleet including An-2s, An-12s, An-24s, An-26s, An-74s, IL-76TDs, Mi-2s, Mi-8s, Tu-154B-2/ Tu-154Ms and Yak-40s is in storage or leased out.

Tu-154B-2 RA-85577 (c/n 83A577) on final approach to Moscow-Domodedovo's runway 14R. As CCCP-85577 it had been operated by the Yakutian CAD/Yakutsk UFD/197th Flight since at least 1987. *Yuriy Kirsanov*

Above: Tu-154M RA-85790 (c/n 93A974) was likewise operated by the Yakutsk Air Enterprise. *Yuriy Kirsanov*

Below: Convertible An-74TK-100 (c/n 365.470.70.655, f/n 0701) was converted from an An-74 *sans suffixe* and can be operated as a freighter or a 32-seater; note the new large emergency exit ahead of the starboard wing. The aircraft belongs to the Kolyma-Indigirka Air Enterprise. *Yuriy Kirsanov*

The state-owned SAT Airlines/Sakhalinskiye Aviatrassy (Sakhalin Air Routes) [HZ/SHU, later GZ/SHU] was established on 20th April 1992, breaking away from the Sakhalin United Air Detachment of the Far Eastern CAD. From its base at Yuzhno-Sakhalinsk (Khomootovo airport) the airline flies scheduled and charter passenger and cargo services to Yuzhno-Kuril'sk, Booreves'nik, Okha, Khabarovsk, Vladivostok, Blagoveschchensk, Hakodate, Seoul and Pusan. The fixed-wing aircraft fleet includes six An-24RVs, three An-26Bs, two de Havilland Canada DHC-8-102 Dash 8s and a single IL-62M (RA-86566, c/n 4255152) shown here; it wears the livery introduced on the carrier's two Boeing 737-200s which have now been returned. The airline also has two Mi-8Ts, three Mi-8MTV-1s and two Kamov Ka-32Ss. *Yuriy Kirsanov*

Samara Airlines

Samara Airlines [E5/BRZ], one of the biggest Russian air carriers, was transformed from the Volga CAD/1st Kuibyshev UAD established in 1961 and comprising the 173rd Flight operating Tu-134As, the 368th Flight operating An-12s, IL-76TDs and Tu-154B-1/B-2/Ms and a further flight operating Yak-40s. The airline operates scheduled and charter domestic and international passenger and cargo services from Samara-Kurumoch. The fleet comprises eight Tu-134As, three Tu-154B-2s, nine Tu-154Ms, three Yak-40s, three Yak-42Ds and three IL-76TDs. The airline was hard hit by the 1998 crisis and the resulting drop in passenger numbers; one of the solutions was the lease off surplus airliners and to develop the cargo transportation activities (which even required additional IL-76s to be leased).

Lit by the setting sun, Samara Airlines Tu-154B-2 RA-85500 (c/n 81A500) is unloaded at Moscow-Domodedovo on 20th November 1998. The aircraft is still in basic Aeroflot colours which look fresh enough but the more recently applied SAMARA titles have all but vanished. *Dmitriy Komissarov*

Seen here taking off at Moscow-Domodedovo in 1997, Tu-154B RA-85150 (c/n 76A150) was one of the oldest Tu-154s operated by Samara Airlines, remaining operational long enough to receive the airline's full livery (the grey-bellied version). The aircraft was retired and broken up at Samara-Kurumoch in January 1998.The Tu-154Ms operated currently have a different version of the livery with a white belly. *Yuriy Kirsanov*

Tu-134A-3 RA-65889 (c/n (53)38010, f/n 3106), one of 15 operated by Samara Airlines, illustrates the initial livery worn by the airline's aircraft. *Yuriy Kirsanov*

Tu-134A-3 RA-65800 (c/n 3352009) is one of the oldest in the fleet. Here it is seen on approach to
Moscow-Domodedovo in the airline's latest livery,
including 'AIRLINES' subtitles. *Yuriy Kirsanov*

Yak-40K RA-87248 (c/n 9540144) wears the grey-bellied version of the full livery and carries the IATA
badge on the centre fuselage. *Dmitriy Petrochenko*

Bought from Vak-Rosat in November 1996, Yak-40
'Salon 2nd Class' RA-88307 (ex Vietnam Airlines
VN-A441, c/n 9421334) was operated for
Rosestbank, as indicated by the additional nose
titles; note the position of the IATA badge on the
engine nacelles. It was sold to Moldavian Airlines
in 1998 as ER-JGD. *Yuriy Kirsanov*

Seen here on a snowbound apron at Samara-Kurumoch, Yak-42D RA-42418 (c/n 4520423219118, f/n 1015) was bought from Samara-based AirVolga (aka Aerovolga), whose overpainted logo is visible on the tail, in 1998. The crudely applied SAMARA airlines titles match the generally shabby appearance of the aircraft. A further example in AirVolga colours (but probably already owned by Samara Airlines) is visible beyond. *Dmitriy Petrochenko*

In contrast, Yak-42 RA-42524 (c/n 11030603) leased from Tsentr Avia in May 2002 and seen here at Samara-Kurumoch shortly thereafter looked immaculate. The multiple grey stripes on the fuselage reveal its origins very clearly. By October 2003 the aircraft had been returned and stripped of Samara Airlines colours. *Dmitriy Petrochenko*

Samara Airlines have three IL-76TDs of their own but these are frequently leased out, forcing the carrier to lease additional IL-76s from other carriers if need arises; in these cases the SAMARA titles and logo are applied to the rear fuselage. Here, RA-76420 (c/n 1023413446, f/n 8702) leased from Almazy Rossiï-Sakha is seen on the cargo apron at Moscow-Domodedovo on the afternoon of 27th November 1998, displaying dual titles. *Dmitriy Komissarov*

Another leased example, IL-76TD RA-76389 leased from Dobrolyot (see page 45), is seen on approach to Moscow-Domodedovo, again sporting both titles. *Yuriy Kirsanov*

Saravia

Saravia (*Saratovskiye avialinii* – Saratov Airlines) [6W/SOV] were formed as the new identity of the Volga CAD/Saratov UAD based at Saratov-Tsentral'nyy and comprising the 171st and 260th Flights operating the An-2/An-24 and Yak-42 respectively, plus a further flight operating Mi-2 helicopters. The airline flies scheduled services and charters within the CIS. The current fleet consists of 11 Yak-42s, one An-24RV and one Mi-2.

Yak-42 RA-42326 (c/n 4520424402154, f/n 0406) seen on approach to Moscow-Domodedovo illustrates the full colour scheme. This aircraft is now on lease to East Line. *Yuriy Kirsanov*

Originally Saravia's Yak-42s were operated in basic Aeroflot colours with the addition of an SA logo and titles. Here, Yak-42D RA-42550 (c/n 11140205) is seen on approach to runway 14R at Moscow-Domodedovo. *Yuriy Kirsanov*

Sibaviatrans

Yak-40K RA-87940 (c/n 9540445) bought from Yeniseyskiy Meridian was operated by Sibaviatrans in 2002. It has since been sold. A Yak-40K registered RA-21503 was the airline's first aircraft. *Dmitriy Petrochenko*

Incorporated on 1st February 1995, Sibaviatrans (aka SIAT) [5M/SIB] operates scheduled domestic and regional services from Krasnoyarsk-Yemel'yanovo airport, as well as passenger charters to various destinations in Europe, SE Asia and the CIS. The current fleet consists of one An-2, seven An-24RVs, one An-32, one An-74-200, one Tu-134A, two Tu-134AKs, one Tu-154B-2, one Mi-2, six Mi-8Ts and three Mi-8MTV-1/Mi-8AMTs.

An-24RV RA-46524 (c/n 47310003) was leased from Kemerovo Avia in 2002 but is no longer in the fleet. Three of SIAT's An-24s are former Romanian aircraft. *Dmitriy Petrochenko*

Bought from Komiinteravia in 1999, radar-nosed Tu-134AK RA-65615 (ex CCCP-65615 No. 2, ex Interflug D-AOBE, ex DDR-SCP, c/n 4352205) was the second of the type operated by Sibaviatrans. It is seen here at Moscow/Vnukovo-1 on 22nd March 2001 with a cap of snow on the nose created by a blizzard a couple of days earlier. By March 2003 the aircraft had been retired. *Dmitriy Komissarov*

Over the years Sibaviatrans operated four Tu-154B-1/B-2s. One of them was Tu-154B-2 RA-85504 leased from Omskavia in June 1999 (see page 80). Since the aircraft was to be leased for one month only, the airline did not take the trouble to repaint it in full SIAT colours, applying only Sibaviatrans titles (which, unusually, were blue, not red). Tu-154B-1 RA-85273 leased from Chernomor-Soyuz in the same time frame was painted identically, except for the Russian flag on the tail and the grey radome. *Yuriy Kirsanov*

Tu-154B-2 RA-85395 (c/n 80A395) was purchased in 2002 from Kolavia; the latter airline had bought the machine from Air Ukraine (specifically, the Kiev-Borispol' division) with which it had flown as UR-85395. Tu-154B-1 RA-85201 and Tu-154M RA-85696 had worn full colours, too. *Yuriy Kirsanov*

Sibir' Airlines

Sibir' Airlines [S7/SBI] were established in 1992 as the successor of the West Siberian CAD/Tolmachovo UAD based at Novosibirsk-Tolmachovo, comprising the 384th Flight (operating Tu-154s and IL-86s) and the 448th Flight (operating An-24s and An-26s). The carrier was losing ground in the early 1990s as a result of the economic downturn in Russia. The change of management in 1998 improved things considerably; in spite of the 1998 crisis Sibir' not only survived but began expanding aggressively, swallowing such carriers as Baikal Airlines and Vnukovo Airlines.

Sibir' Airlines exhibit a variety of colour schemes which is due partly to the different origins of its aircraft. Seen here at Moscow/Vnukovo-1 on 29th May 2000 Tu-154B-2 RA-85402 (c/n 80A402) displays the first own livery combining the old Aeroflot cheatline with the 'Blue Forest' tail colours. It still looked like this in December 2003. *Dmitriy Komissarov*

Besides Novosibirsk, the airline has bases in Moscow and Irkutsk. Currently Sibir' operates scheduled services throughout the CIS and charters to Europe, the Middle East and Africa with one An-26, ten Tu-154B-1/B-2s, 26 Tu-154Ms, two Tu-204-100s and 14 IL-86s. Sibir' has interline agreements with Air China, Asiana, Korean Air, Lufthansa and Uzbekistan Airways.

Also depicted at Moscow/Vnukovo-1 on 29th May 2000, Tu-154B-2 RA-85495 (c/n 81A495) illustrates the first full colour scheme utilised by Sibir' – specifically, the white-bellied variety which combines the same tail colours with a new cheatline. Like RA-85402, this aircraft was inherited from the West Siberian CAD/Tolmachovo UFD/384th Flight. *Dmitriy Komissarov*

The Tu-154M is numerically the most important type operated by Sibir'. Here two of these aircraft, with RA-85699 (c/n 91A874) in the foreground, are seen undergoing routine maintenance at Novosibirsk-Tolmachovo. Both aircraft wear the white-bellied version of the old full livery. *RART*

Sibir' acquired a considerable number of Tu-154Ms from the defunct Vnukovo Airlines. One of them, RA-85619 (c/n 86A738), is named *Yulia Fomina* in memory of a stewardess killed in the line of duty on this very aircraft when it was hijacked by Chechen terrorists while still owned by Vnukovo Airlines. *Dmitriy Petrochenko*

A dramatic nighttime shot of Tu-154M RA-85620 (c/n 86A739) at Irkutsk-1 in late 2002, with RA-85687 (90A857) in the background. Here the origins of the aircraft are obvious because RA-85620 retains the basic livery of Vnukovo Airlines complete with the VA tail logo. Two other ex-Vnukovo Airlines examples (RA-85615 and RA-85673) wear Russian Aviation Consortium colours (see page 155). *Dmitriy Petrochenko*

Another curious hybrid. Tu-154M RA-85652 (c/n 89A794) acquired in 2001 retains the striking livery of the late Baikal Airlines, including the tail logo representing a gull over the waters of Lake Baikal, but wears Sibir' titles. Note the green badge on the grey belly with the legend *Sto shest'desyat let Sberbanku Rossiï* (Savings Bank of Russia 160 years); the bank, which was founded in 1841, is one of the airline's strategic partners. *Yuriy Kirsano*

IL-86 RA-86089 (c/n 51483206060) was also acquired from Vnukovo Airlines in 2001 and likewise sports the 'Savings Bank of Russia 160 years' badge. *Yuriy Kirsanov*

Seen here at Novosibirsk-Tolmachovo in 2001, IL-86 RA-86105 (c/n 51483208073) was the first Sibir' aircraft to receive the early-standard full colour scheme. Sister ship RA-86109 has a slightly different livery, the cheatline proper and the curved pinstripes-cum-fir-tree having the same dark blue colour. *Dmitriy Petrochenko*

Sibir' operates two Tu-204-100s which were acquired second hand from Vnukovo Airlines (RA-64011) and leased from the Aviastar factory (RA-64017). One of the two is seen here retracting its undercarriage after take-off. *RART*

Sibir' inherited four An-26s from the 448th Flight, including RA-26563 (c/n 3506). This was the sole example remaining by 2002, shown here sitting in storage at Novosibirsk-Tolmachovo with a support under its tail. The aircraft still wears full Aeroflot colours supplemented by Sibir' titles under the registration. *Dmitriy Petrochenko*

In mid-2003 Sibir' introduced a new livery with a completely white fuselage and bold white titles on the tail sporting a modified version of the 'Blue Forest' colours. Several Tu-154Ms have already been repainted according to the latest fashion, including RA-85610, RA-85612, RA-85623 and RA-85709. The latter aircraft (c/n 91A884) depicted here was probably the first to be thus repainted. *Dmitriy Petrochenko*

Sirius-Aero

Sirius Aero [–/CIG] was established in 1999 as a business charter operator based at Moscow/Vnukovo-1, initially flying a single Tu-134AK (RA-65550) leased from the Ivanovo State Air Enterprise. In 2000 it was returned and replaced by Tu-134A 'Salon' RA-65653 (c/n 0351009) leased from the Novosibirsk-based Siberian Aviation Research Institute (SibNIA); this was the oldest operational example at the time. Here it is shown at Moscow/Vnukovo-1 on 29th May 2000 as originally operated in basic Aeroflot colours with Cyrillic Sirius-Aero titles and no flag; the 'whitewall tyres' on the nose gear unit are noteworthy. By August 2001 RA-65653 had received an all-white corporate colour scheme with triple blue pinstripes and no titles; it was finally retired in 2003. *Dmitriy Komissarov*

Tu-134A-3 'Salon' RA-65794 (c/n (03)63135, f/n 5605), a former Voronezhavia aircraft leased from the Rostov aircraft overhaul plant by June 2000, wears large Cyrillic titles and the yellow-underlined cheatline of the former operator. *Yuriy Kirsanov*

Tu-134A-3M RA-65928 (c/n (63)66491, f/n 6372), was bought from the Ivanovo State Air Enterprise as a Tu-134SKh in late 2001 and converted by January 2002, receiving this anonymous corporate-style livery also worn by Tu-134A 'Salon' RA-65653 and Tu-134AK RA-65880. Note the different window arrangement as compared to RA-65725 on page 79 – small wonder, since all Tu-134A-3Ms were converted in accordance with the differing requirements of their respective buyers. *Dmitriy Komissarov*

Sirius-Aero also operates aircraft for other enterprises. For example, two more Tu-134A-3Ms, RA-65723 and RA-65724 (both converted from ex-Voronezhavia Tu-134SKh's), are operated for S-Air Service in this pleasing three-tone blue colour scheme. The latter aircraft (c/n (63)66445, f/n 6370) is depicted here at Moscow/Vnukovo-1 on 6th May 2003. RA-65723 is absolutely identical, except that it retains the tall strake aerial of the A-723 LORAN. Again, note the difference in window arrangement as compared to RA-65725. As of this writing, Sirius Aero has four Tu-134A-3Ms, two Tu-134AKs and one Tu-134A. 'Salon'.

Sirius-Aero also operates a single Yak-40, RA-87669 (formerly EW-65669 withe Belair, ex-Polish Air Force '049 Red', c/n 9021760). It is depicted here at Moscow/Vnukovo-1 on 29th May 2000. *Both Dmitriy Komissarov*

Spetsavia

As the Bykovo-Avia airline broke up in 1999, part of it became a new entity called Spetsavia (= Special Air). The enterprise performs navaids calibration work with a single An-24ALK and three An-26ASLKs. One of the latter, RA-26631 (c/n 5503), is seen here in the static park of the Civil Aviation-2002 airshow at Moscow-Domo-dedovo. Note the fairing under the nose housing a powerful retractable light for phototheodolite measurements.

Dmitriy Komissarov

Sukhoi Aircompany

Sukhoi Aircompany [–/SUH], a subsidiary of the Sukhoi Design Bureau, Russia's famous 'fighter maker', operated mostly IL-76s leased as required. These included IL-76TD 'Falsie' RA-76659 leased from Atruvera Airlines. No IL-76s are operated at present. *Yuriy Kirsanov*

Sukhoi Aircompany also operates two Yak-40Ks and a Tu-134A-3 'Salon' as corporate transports and support aircraft. RA-98111 (c/n 9741656) is shown here at Ghelendjik in September 1999. The other Yak-40 (RA-87229) is marked in identical fashion to the IL-76 above. *Yefim Gordon*

Tatarstan Air

The Yak-42 was the main type operated by the old Tatarstan Airlines' 1st Kazan' Air Enterprise after the 261st Flight transitioned to the type from the Tu-134A, and it still is the 'new' Tatarstan Air's most important type. Here, immaculate Yak-42 RA-42332 (c/n 4520421605135, f/n 1006) with 'Avialinii Tatarstana' titles/logo and the Tatatrstan flag awaits redelivery to the owner at Moscow-Bykovo on 8th April 1993 after an overhaul at the Aircraft Repair Plant No. 402. *Dmitriy Komissarov*

The Republic of Tatarstan's flag carrier has an interesting history. In early 1993 most of the republic's flight detachments were merged into the Avialinii Tatarstana (Tatarstan Airlines) state company. In 1997, however, this disintegrated into four separate companies – the Bugul'ma Air Enterprise [–/BGM], the First Kazan' Air Enterprise [–/KAZ], the Nizhnekamsk Air Enterprise [–/NKM] and the Second Kazan' Air Enterprise performing commuter flights and utility work.

In 1999 the republican government decided that a new national air carrier should be formed. Thus the First Kazan' AE, the Nizhnekamsk AE and Begishevo airport serving Naberezhnyye Chelny and Nizhnekamsk reunited into the Tatarstan Air Joint-Stock Co. [U9/KAZ], a 100% state-owned enterprise. So far the Bugul'ma AE with its fleet of Yak-40s and the Second Kazan' AE remain independent.

Tatarstan Air flies domestic passenger schedules and charters from Kazan to Moscow and St. Petersburg. The fleet consists of four An-24RVs, one An-26, two Tu-134As, two Tu-134AKs, three Tu-154B-2s, two Tu-154Ms and nine Yak-42s.

Opposite page:

A newer Yak-42D, RA-42433 (c/n 4520421301017), takes off from runway 14L at Moscow-Domodedovo in 2000, showing Tatarstan Air's original livery. Other examples, such as RA-42333, wore the all-white version with the Tatarstan flag on the tail which was later replaced by the winged lion logo. *Yuriy Kirsanov*

In 1999 Tatarstan Air introduced the Tu-134A, a type that had not been operated in the republic since the mid-1980s. Here, Tu-134AK RA-65691 (c/n (03)63195, f/n 5703) leased from Volga-Aviaexpress in December 2000 and subsequently bought, takes off from runway 14R at Moscow-Domodedovo, showing the airline's current livery. The winged lion is part of the Kazan' city crest. *Yuriy Kirsanov*

The First Kazan' Air Enterprise of Tatarstan Air operates three Tu-154B-2s, including this example with the out-of-sequence registration RA-85804 (ex Cargo Moravia Airlines OK-LCS, ex Czech Federal Government Flight OK-BYC, c/n 81A517) which should have been RA-85517. The aircraft wears all-white colours with TATARSTAN titles and Tatarstan/Russian flags. *Yuriy Kirsanov*

Originally much of the 'first-generation' Tatarstan Airlines' fleet retained Aeroflot titles and logos with the Tatarstan flag on the tail in lieu of the Soviet flag, as illustrated here by Bugul'ma Air Enterprise Yak-40 RA-87404 (c/n 9411633) at Moscow-Bykovo on 8th April 1993. *Dmitriy Komissarov*

This page:

Below: An-24RV RA-47804 (c/n 17306903), a converted An-24B, starts up the engines at Moscow-Domodedovo on the morning of 3rd November 1998, displaying *Nizhnekamskoye aviapredpriyatiye* (Nizhnekamsk Air Enterprise) titles and logo; the enterprise has now been reintegrated into Tatarstan Air. A couple of minutes after the aircraft taxied out for take-off from runway 32L a malfunction occurred, forcing the flight to be delayed. *Dmitriy Komissarov*

Top: Tatarstan Airlines operated Western jets for a while as government transports. One was a Lockheed L-1329 JetStar II (N341K); the other was this Boeing 727-193, P4-JLD (c/n 19620, f/n 377) leased from Joylud Distributors International (originally delivered as VR-CWC in September 1993 on lease from Pinecroft). Both aircraft were returned in 1998. *Yuriy Kirsanov*

Above: First Kazan' Air Enterprise An-24B RA-46338 (c/n 97305606) in Avialinii Tatarstana (Tatarstan Airlines) colours makes an afternoon approach to Moscow-Bykovo. This aircraft was retired by 1999. *Yuriy Kirsanov*

Tavia, alias Taganrog Aviation [–/TGR], was formed in 1995, operating a small fleet consisting of two An-24RVs (RA-46419 and RA-46491) and one An-26 (RA-26195). The aircraft are regularly used in support of the Taganrog-based Beriyev Aviation Scientific & Technical Complex (TANTK imeni Beriyeva). Here, one of the airline's An-24s sits on the grass at Ghelendjik in September 1999. *Yefim Gordon*

Tesis

Established in 1992, Tesis [UZ/TIS] started operations from Moscow with a single IL-76TD. The fleet was progressively expanded with other IL-76TDs – mostly leased as required. Tesis operates domestic and international cargo charters to destinations including China, India, the UAE and Turkey, as well as passenger charters to Cyprus and Egypt. The current fleet includes six IL-76TDs and two Tu-154B-2s operated in a combi configuration. Here, one of the airline's own IL-76TDs, RA-76380 No. 2 (converted from Ukrainian Air Force IL-76MD UR-76561, c/n 0033447364, f/n 3501) in 2002, is unloaded at Moscow/Vnukovo-1 on 6th May 2003. The original RA-76380 (c/n 1033418578, f/n 9005) had been sold to the Yemeni Air Force in 1995 as 7O-ADF.
Dmitriy Komissarov

Titan Aero

Titan Aero Joint-Stock Co. [–/RTT] was founded in 1999. The carrier operates passenger and cargo charters from Moscow-Vnukovo and Zhukovskiy with a single ex-Ilavia IL-18V (RA-75834) and two IL-76TDs.

One of Titan Aero's two IL-76TDs, RA-76493 (c/n 0043456700, f/n 4305), sits at Moscow/Vnu-kovo-1 on 6th May 2003. The aircraft is leased from the Voronezh aircraft factory (VASO) and sports large Titan Aero titles but no logo.
Dmitriy Komissarov

Titan-Aero's other IL-76TD, RA-76822 (c/n 0093499982, f/n 7506) pictured on the same day at the same location, wears Titan Aero titles so small they are hardly discernible at all. Leased from Abakan-Avia, this aircraft has quite a history. Originally built as an IL-76MD 'Falsie', the aircraft was operated by the Ilyushin OKB, taking part in a much-publicised airlift operation to the Antarctica in August 1991 to pick up a crew of Soviet researchers from Ice Station Molodyozhnaya. The aircraft changed its identity to an IL-76TD after being repainted in Ilavia colours; later it received this colour scheme, except that 'AK imeni Ilyushina' (Ilyushin Aircraft Complex) titles and a large Ilyushin badge were carried until the aircraft was sold. *Dmitriy Komissarov*

Tomsk-Avia

Established 1992 as the successor of the West Siberian CAD/Tomsk UAD/119th Flight based at Tomsk-Bogashevo, Tomsk Avia absorbed the Kolpashevo Air Enterprise in 1999. The carrier operates domestic passenger and cargo scheduled and charter services as an associate company of Sibir' Airlines. The fleet consists of one An-24B, five An-24RVs, two An-26s, eleven former Kolpashevo Air Enterprise An-28s, five Yak-40s, seven Mi-2s, 57 Mi-8Ts and four Mi-8MTV-1s. The few remaining Tu-154B-2s have been sold to Sibir'.

Tomsk Avia Tu-154B-2 RA-85485 (c/n 81A485) is seen at Moscow-Domodedovo on 20th September 1998, shortly before sale to Sibir'.
Dmitriy Komissarov

The airline often operates its aircraft in the interests of oil and natural gas companies. Here, Yak-40 'Salon 2nd Class' RA-87494 (c/n 9541745) is seen at Krasnoyarsk-Yemenl'yanovo in 2002, wearing the attractive livery of Vostokgazprom (= East Gas Industry) with additional Tomsk Avia titles and logo. Note the different style of the titles.
Dmitriy Petrochenko

Transaero

Initially Transaero operated Tu-154Ms in basic Aeroflot colours with red Cyrillic ТРАНСАЭРО titles. The first aircraft to receive the now-familiar livery (which bears more than a passing resemblance to that of Air France) was IL-86 CCCP-86123 (later RA-86123) named *Moskva* (Moscow). This aircraft is now on lease to VASO Airlines, having been previously leased to Kras Air. *Yuriy Kirsanov*

Established on 28th December 1990 and starting operations on 5th November 1991, Moscow/Sheremet'yevo-based Transaero [4J/TSO, later UN/TSO] was one of the first new airlines breaking away from Aeroflot (its first aircraft still had the old Soviet prefix). Originally operating Soviet-built aircraft leased from Aeroflot and the Soviet/Russian Air Force (including the Tu-154M, the Tu-154C freighter, the An-124 Ruslan and even the Mi-8MTV assault helicopter), Transaero was also one of the first Soviet airlines to order Western equipment, leasing an initial two Boeing 737-2C9s in 1991, and two Boeing 757-2Y0s in 1992.

The first international service (Moscow to Tel Aviv) was inaugurated in November 1993. The carrier soon made its mark as a strong competitor to Aeroflot Russian International Airlines. True, the airline did suffer heavily from the 1998 crisis, dropping from second place to seventh in the top 20 list as regards passenger numbers by May 1999, but has recovered since then.

Today Transaero has scheduled and charter flights to more than 20 domestic and international destinations, including London, Frankfurt/Main, Paphos and Strasbourg. The carrier has alliances with Air Moldova and KrasAir. The airline's oper-

ating base was moved to Moscow-Domodedovo on 24th April 2001.

Currently Transaero has an all-Boeing fleet of three 737-200s, two 737-300s, two 737-700s, three 767-200ERs and three 767-300ERs; the sole IL-86 has been leased off. A single Airbus A310-300 was briefly operated, too. True, the carrier is not opposed to indigenous hardware; plans to buy six IL-96M long-range widebodies with delivery in 2001-02 were foiled by the crisis. Later Transaero ordered ten Tu-204-100s but that order has now been converted to the short-fuselage/long-range Tu-204-300 for which Transaero is the launch customer.

Boeing 737-236 Advanced YL-BAB *Tat'yana* (ex British Airways G-BGJK, c/n 22032, f/n 742) was leased from Finavion in June 1994 and jointly operated with charter carrier Riga Airlines (RiAir). The alliance came to an end when RiAir suspended operations in January 1999. *Yuriy Kirsanov*

Transaero's first two Boeing 737s were registered RA-73000 and RA-73001, later moving to the Irish register as EI-CLN and EI-CLO respectively at the insistence of the lessor. Now, however, three 737-200s have reverted to the Russian register – and, confusingly, these are different aircraft. Here, RA-73001 No. 2 is shown at Moscow-Domodedovo on 17th August 2002. This is not the original Boeing 737-2C9 Advanced (c/n 21444, f/n 516) but a Boeing 737-236 Advanced (c/n 22028, f/n 656) which was formerly operated as YL-BAA *Riga* (ex-BA G-BGJG)! The aircraft is now named *Aleksandr* – probably as a hint to Transaero's former CEO Aleksandr Pleshakov. *Dmitriy Komissarov*

At one time Transaero briefly operated this Boeing 737-2K3 Advanced, YU-ANU (c/n 24139, f/n 1530) leased from the Yugoslav charter carrier Aviogenex in the latter's colours. *Yuriy Kirsanov*

In May and June 1998 Transaero took delivery of two Boeing 737-7K9s leased from Bavaria International Aircraft leasing. The first of two, N100UN (the last two letters are obviously a hint at the carrier's UN flight code; c/n 28088, f/n 19) is seen here on finals to Moscow-Sheremet'yevo shortly after delivery, as indicated by the fact that the aircraft is still nameless (it was christened *Bavaria* soon afterwards). Transaero is the sole operator of the Boeing 737NG in the CIS. *Dmitriy Petrochenko*

Exactly four years later, in May and June 2002, Transaero took delivery of two ex-Sabena Boeing 737-329s. The second of these, EI-CXR (ex OO-SYA, c/n 24355, f/n 1709) is illustrated here; both of these aircraft are still nameless as of this writing. *Dmitriy Petrochenko*

Seen here on approach to Moscow-Sheremet'yevo, Boeing 757-2Y0 EI-CJY *Novosibirsk* (c/n 26161, f/n 557) was the second of the type delivered; it was leased from GPA Group in April 1994. The aircraft was sold to GE Capital as N161GE while still operated by Transaero and returned in 1998. *Yuriy Kirsanov*

In June 1996 Transaero also briefly operated three former American Airlines McDonnell Douglas DC-10-30s leased from the Finavion leasing company. This is the third aircraft, N142AA (c/n 46714, f/n 167) named *Aleksey Lozovoy*; the An-24 style registration RA-46714 was allocated for this aircraft but not taken up. The other two were N140AA and N141AA which were to have been reregistered RA-46712 and RA-46713 respectively. All three were returned in 1998. *Yuriy Kirsanov*

Transaero took delivery of its first 767 in March 1998; it was Boeing 767-3Q8ER N601LF (c/n 28206, f/n 694) leased from ILFC and returned 1998. Pictured here is one of the 767-200s delivered later. *Dmitriy Petrochenko*

Boeing 767-216ER EI-CZD (c/n 23623, f/n 142) taxies at Moscow-Domodedovo. *Dmitriy Petrochenko*

In 2002-03 Transaero received more 767s, including Boeing 767-3Q8ER EI-DBF (c/n 24745, f/n 355). *Dmitriy Petrochenko*

Tsentr-Avia (ex Bykovo Avia)

The first livery worn by Bykovo-Avia's Yak-42s when the airline assumed its own identity was this colour scheme with 'Russian flag' tail stripes. The silver-coloured titles were pretty hard to read from certain angles. This is RA-42341 (c/n 4520421706292, f/n 0907) approaching its home base in 1995. *Yuriy Kirsanov*

The carrier started life in 1993 as Bykovo Avia [–/BKU]; this was the new identity of the Central Regions CAD/Bykovo UAD based at Moscow's smallest airport and consisting of two Flights which operated a mix of An-24s and An-26s (the 61st Flight) and Yak-42 short-haul trijets respectively.

The 1998 bank crisis and the ensuing drop in passenger traffic took a heavy toll on the airline. Bykovo had always had the air of a quiet provincial airport with comparatively little traffic, and things became especially quiet in late 1998 and 1999 in the wake of the bank crisis. In order to survive the carrier underwent a major reorganisation in 1999, the Yak-42 flight emerging under the new name of Tsentr-Avia (Centre-Avia) [J7/CVC]. The An-26 flight became a separate entity (see Spetsavia, page 104), the elderly An-24s having been retired or sold by 1998.

Initially operating scheduled flights (to Magnitogorsk in the north and Ghelendjik in the south) and weekly charters to Hanover, Stuttgart and Leipzig in its own name and to Noyabr'sk for Gazpromavia from Bykovo, Tsentr-Avia shifted its main base to Moscow-Domodedovo in 2001. The three Yak-40s operated in 1999-2000 are no longer in the fleet which now consists of a single An-24RV (RA-46665, which is not one of the original 61st Flight machines) and seven Yak-42s, a further three having been sold. Tsentr-Avia has strong ties with the *Aviatekhnologiya* (= aviation technology) leasing company and the Bykovo Aircraft Services Company (BASCO) which overhauls the Yak-42.

The same aircraft in 1999, now wearing the carrier's second livery (dubbed 'The Flying Bull'). The tail logo is logical enough, since *byk* is Russian for 'bull'. *Yuriy Kirsanov*

RA-42549 (c/n 11140105) illustrates the basic Tsentr-Avia livery introduced in 1999. Part of the fleet wore this all-white scheme. *Yuriy Kirsanov*

In contrast, some Tsentr-Avia Yak-42s, such as RA-42378 (c/n 4520421014494, f/n 0811) have a grey belly and grey stripes along the fuselage. *Yuriy Kirsanov*

Yak-42D RA-42368 (c/n 4520422914166, f/n 0610) has been outfitted as an executive jet for the Magnitogorsk Metal Foundry (MMK – *Magnitogorskiy metallurgicheskiy kombinaht*). It is seen here in the static park of the Civil Aviation-2002 airshow at Moscow-Domodedovo, with a large logo marking the operator's 70th anniversary; note the satellite communications antenna blister. *Dmitriy Komissarov*

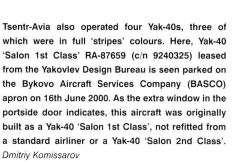

Tsentr-Avia also operated four Yak-40s, three of which were in full 'stripes' colours. Here, Yak-40 'Salon 1st Class' RA-87659 (c/n 9240325) leased from the Yakovlev Design Bureau is seen parked on the Bykovo Aircraft Services Company (BASCO) apron on 16th June 2000. As the extra window in the portside door indicates, this aircraft was originally built as a Yak-40 'Salon 1st Class', not refitted from a standard airliner or a Yak-40 'Salon 2nd Class'. *Dmitriy Komissarov*

Tsentr-Yoog (Centre-South)

Established in 1990, Tsentr-Yoog (aka Centre-South) [–/CTS] is the other airline based in Belgorod. The entire fleet consists of two Yak-40 'Salon 2nd Class' executive jets, only one of which wears the airline's livery.

Yak-40 'Salon 2nd Class' RA-87550 (c/n 9210121) taxies at Moscow-Vnukovo in the mid-1990s; the titles had been removed by March 2001. The airline's other aircraft, RA-87467, is in basic Aeroflot colours without titles. *Yuriy Kirsanov*

223rd Flight Unit

The Russian Air Force has commercial divisions, one of which is the 223rd Flight Unit State Airline based at Chkalovskaya airbase east of Moscow. The airline's fleet comprises one An-12BP, four IL-18D/Es, five IL-62Ms, five IL-76MDs, five Tu-134AKs and ten Tu-154B-2s; some of the airliners are staff transports. Here, 168-seat IL-62M RA-86496 (c/n 3829859) is seen on finals to Moscow-Vnukovo's runway 24 on 17th March 2002. *Dmitriy Komissarov*

224th Flight Unit

The other commercial division of the Russian Air Force is the 224th Flight Unit State Airline [–/TTF]. It comprises airlift units based at Tver'-2 (Migalovo) AB and Bryansk-2 (Seshcha) AB operating IL-76MDs and An-124s respectively. The fleet changes constantly, the aircraft being assigned to the airline on a rotation basis. Originally flown in pure Aeroflot colours, some aircraft later received small round blue badges on the tail with the numerals 224. One sich aircraft, IL-76MD RA-76669 (c/n 0063465949, f/n 4908), an Afghan war veteran, seen lifting off from runway 24 at Moscow-Vnukovo which, along with Zhukovskiy, is one of the airline's main operating bases. *Yuriy Kirsanov*

Some of the aircraft, including IL-76MD RA-76719 (c/n 0073474226, f/n 5607) seen here at Moscow/Vnukovo-1 on 5th September 2001, combine the '224' badge with Aeroflot titles/logo. At least one aircraft (RA-78834) has received large 224-Й ЛЁТНЫЙ ОТРЯД (*Dvesti dvadtsat' chetvyortyy lyotnyy otryad* – 224th Flight Unit) titles on the forward fuselage in mid-1999. The 224th Flight Unit's aircraft have participated in the airlift operation in support of the Russian contingent of the Kosovo Stabilisation Force (KFOR). *Dmitriy Komissarov*

Tulpar

The Kazan'-based Tulpar Aviation Co. [–/TUL] (the name means 'winged steed' in Tatarian) was established in 1991, operating scheduled and charter passenger services (among other things, for petroleum companies). The current fleet comprises five Yak-40s, six Yak-42Ds and one Mi-8T. In 2003 Tulpar was set to merge with Karat, with which it has an alliance.

Yak-40 'Salon 2nd Class' RA-87496 (c/n 9541945), seen here at Moscow/Vnukovo-1 on 4th October 2000, is operated for Nizhnekamsk-neftekhim (Nizhnekamsk Petroleum Chemistry Co.). *Dmitriy Komissarov*

Yak-40 'Salon 1st Class' RA-87503 (c/n 9510240) wore a slightly different livery. *Yuriy Kirsanov*

Seen here taxiing in at Kazan'-Osnovnoy airport in December 2000, Tu-134A 'Salon' RA-65079 (ex LY-ASK, c/n (73)60054, f/n 4206) retained the basic white/grey/red colours of ex-owner Aurela Co. with Tulpar titles. In January 2001 the aircraft was sold to Avcom (see page 25). *Il'dar valeyev*

Another aircraft which is no longer operated is Yak-40 'Salon 2nd Class' RA-98113 (c/n 9710253) seen here at Moscow/Vnukovo-1 on 22nd March 2001 in basic Airstan colours. This aircraft later went to Karat (see page 66). *Dmitriy Komissarov*

Resplendent in Tulpar colours, Yak-42D RA-42425 (c/n 4520423303016) is seen here moments after touching down in Moscow-Vnukovo's runway 06. This aircraft has been leased to Kish Air as EP-LAH and, more recently, to Cubana as CU-T1243. *Yuriy Kirsanov*

Tura Air Enterprise

Based at Tura in the Krasnoyarsk Region, the Tura Air Enterprise (formerly the Krasnoyarsk CAD/Tura UAD) operates a mix of types, including two An-2s, two An-3Ts, one An-26B-100, one An-32, seven Mi-8Ts, three Mi-8MTV-1s and one Yak-40 (RA-87900, c/n 9720254). The latter aircraft is depicted at Krasnoyarsk-Yemel'yanovo in 2002, showing off its attractive colour scheme with Evenkia titles. *Dmitriy Petrochenko*

Tuva Airlines

Tuva Airlines (Tuvinskiye Avialinii) based in Kyzyl is the national air carrier of the Republic of Tuva providing regional air transportation and air services. The fleet comprises ten An-2s, five Mi-8s and nine Yak-40s. One of the latter, RA-88212 (c/n 9631849), is seen here at Krasnoyarsk-Yemel'yanovo in 2002. *Dmitriy Petrochenko*

Ural Airlines

Based in Yekaterinburg (formerly Sverdlovsk), Ural Airlines/*Ooral'skiye avialinii* [U6/SVR] were formed on 28th December 1993 when the Urals CAD/1st Sverdlovsk UAD was separated from Kol'tsovo airport. Since then Ural Airlines have become one of Russia's major air carriers, operating domestic and international flights to more than 40 countries in Asia and Europe. The current fleet comprises three An-24Bs, three IL-86s, twelve Tu-154B-2s and four Tu-154Ms, the three An-2Bs having been retired.

The Tu-154B-2 is Ural Airlines' most numerous type, though the newer Tu-154Ms are usually operated on flights abroad. RA-85508 (c/n 81A508) illustrates the livery with the logo representing the stylised Cyrillic letters UA on the nose and tail. *Above, S. and D. Komissarov collection; below, Yuriy Kirsanov*

RA-86078 (c/n 51483205049) may be the oldest of Ural Airlines' three IL-86s but it looks magnificent all the same, gleaming with fresh paint after a recent overhaul. Here it is seen a second before touchdown on runway 14L at Moscow-Domodedovo. *Yuriy Kirsanov*

UTair (ex Tyumen'aviatrans)

Founded in 1991 as Tyumen'aviatrans [P2/TMN], this is the largest airline operating in the oil-rich Tyumen' region of Siberia. On 1st October 2002 the airline was rebranded UTair – partly because its activities were not limited to the Tyumen' Region, partly because foreigners had trouble pronouncing the old name.

The carrier has three main bases – Tyumen' (Plekhanovo airport), Khanty-Mansiysk and Surgut (Pobedit airport) – and a huge fleet with widely varied aircraft. As of April 2003 the fixed-wing aircraft oper-

ated are 47 An-2s, 11 An-24B/RVs, 16 Tu-134A/AKs leased from other carriers as required, two Tu-154B-2s, nine Tu-154Ms and 22 Yak-40s. The airline is also Russia's largest helicopter operator with 116 Mi-8Ts and 'Ps, eight Mi-6As, seven Mi-10Ks and 19 Mi-26Ts. Unlike some other Russian carriers, Tyumenaviatrans sticks to indigenous equipment, the only exception being a Gulfstream IVSP business jet operated for the Surgutneftegaz petroleum company. The carrier has its own training centre with simulators.

UTair owns several large airports, including Noyabr'sk which was originally built to serve the Noyabr'skoye oil field but now enjoys federal status. UTair operates scheduled and charter passenger and cargo services both in Russia and abroad. Additionally, Tyumenaviatrans and now UTair undertakes a lot of air services under contracts from the United Nations Organisation, operating relief flights in areas hit by natural disasters or military conflicts.

Tyumen'AviaTrans Tu-154M RA-85813 (c/n 95A990) touches down at Moscow-Vnukovo. For many years the airline's aircraft wore basic Aeroflot colours. *Yuriy Kirsanov*

Tu-154M RA-85805 (c/n 94A986) awaiting the next flight at Moscow/Vnukovo-1 on 29th May 2000 illustrates the full livery worn by many Tyumen'aviatrans aircraft. Some of the Tu-154Ms had names; for instance, RA-85820 was christened *Roman Marchenko*. *Dmitriy Komissarov*

RA-85733 (c/n 92A915), a former Murmansk Airlines Tu-154M named *Antonina Grigor'yeva* is depicted at Moscow/Vnukovo-1 on 5th September 2001, carrying the 'Yugra' crest on the tail; the same emblem is worn by RA-85755 *Vasiliy Bakhilov*, another ex-Murmansk Airlines aircraft. *Dmitriy Komissarov*

Close-up of the elaborate 'Yugra' crest on RA-85733. Yugra is the ancient name of the Khanty-Mansi Autonomous District; since Khanty-Mansiysk is one of the carrier's main bases, it is logical that their crest should be applied. *Dmitriy Komissarov*

RA-87240 (c/n 9530743), one of the many Yak-40s operated by Tyumen'aviatrans, comes in to land. Most aircraft wore Cyrillic titles, although at least one Yak-40 is known to have had English titles. *Yuriy Kirsanov*

An-24RV RA-46481 (c/n 27308009) sits at Tyumen'-Plekhanovo in full Tyumen'aviatrans colours in 2002, with ex-Baikalavia Tu-154M RA-85613 in the background. *Dmitriy Petrochenko*

Tyumen'aviatrans (UTair) actively leases Tu-134s from other carriers. Here, Tu-134A-3 RA-65049 (ex Gomelavia EW-65049, c/n (73)49755, f/n 3808) is seen parked at Moscow/Vnukovo-1 on 6th May 2003. Despite the fact that the aircraft was leased from Orenburg Airlines in December 2002 (ie, after the name change), it still wears the old Tyumen'aviatrans titles. Note the wide unpainted fin leading edge usually found on late-production Tu-134AKs. *Dmitriy Komissarov*

Tu-134A-3 RA-65083 (c/n (73)60090, f/n 4210) was leased from AVL Arkhangel'sk Airlines in June 2002, being the second Tu-134 to wear the full colours of Tyumen'aviatrans. *Yuriy Kirsanov*

Seen in the static park of the Civil Aviation 2002 airshow at Moscow-Domodedovo on 15th August 2002, this Mi-26T with the out-of-sequence registration RA-06078 (c/n 34001212045) is a former Ukrainian Air Force machine bought in 2002, as revealed by the chaff/flare packs on the fuselage characteristic of military examples. Note the titles reading *Ours is the largest*. *Dmitriy Komissarov*

The same RA-65083 in its current guise at Moscow/Vnukovo-1 on 6th May 2003. This was the first Tu-134 to gain full UTair titles.
Dmitriy Komissarov

Seen at the same location on the same date, Tu-154M RA-85727 (c/n 92A909) is the most recent addition to the fleet, having flown with ELK Estonian Airways until 2002 as ES-LTP. Unlike some other UTair aircraft, it has Tyumen'aviatrans-style colours with a blue side flash. *Dmitriy Komissarov*

Vyborg North-Western Air Transport Co.

The Vyborg North-Western Air Transport Co. (*Severo-Zapadnaya aviatrahnsport-naya kompaniya Vyborg*) [–VBG] started operations in 2002 from St. Petersburg-Pulkovo with two Mi-8Ts and two ex-Uzbekistan Airways IL-114s, with three brand-new examples on order. Here IL-114 RA-91015 (formerly UK 91000, c/n 1013828025, f/n 0107) is seen in the static display at the MAKS-2003 airshow on 22nd August 2003; it has a stylish interior with an in-flight entertainment system.

VASO Airlines [–/VSO] is the flying division of the Voronezh Aircraft Production Joint-Stock Co. (VASO – *Voronezhskoye aktsionernoye samolyotostroitel'noye obschchestvo*), the former MAP aircraft factory No. 64, which currently produces the IL-96-300 long-haul airliner. Apart from supporting the operations of the factory itself, the airline flies passenger charters with a single An-24RV bearing the non-standard registration RA-48096 (c/n 57310406) and two IL-86; for a while it even operated scheduled flights under the DN flight code. The sole IL-76TD has been leased to Titan Aero. *Yuriy Kirsanov*

The charter carrier Vim Airlines [–/MOV] started operations in 2002, breaking away from Aerofreight Airlines (see page 132) after a row withi the management. 'Vim' are the initials of the airline's director, Viktor I. Merkoolov. The fleet comprises four An-12B/BP freighters and five IL-62Ms in combi configuration, four of which are former Aeroflot Russian Airlines aircraft. The fifth is RA-86935 (ex-CSA Czech Airlines OK-PBM, c/n 1545951), seen here at Moscow/Vnukovo-1 on 6th May 2003. It was named *Natal'ya* (Nathalie) after purchase by its original Russian owner, Rusavia-Charter, in 2000. *Dmitriy Komissarov*

Vladikavkaz Air Enterprise

The Vladikavkaz Air Enterprise [–/OSV] is the other airline based in the capital of North Osetia (Alania). Once again this is a small enterprise, the entire fleet consisting of two Yak-40s and a single Mi-8MTV-1. One of the two jets, Yak-40 'Salon 2nd Class' RA-87569 (c/n 9220222), is seen during one of its frequent visits to Moscow/Vnukovo-1 on 18th June 2002. *Dmitriy Komissarov*

Vladivostok Air

Vladivostok Air [XF/VLK] is the new identity of the Far Eastern CAD/Vladivostok UAD based at Vladivostok-Knevichi. Established in 1992, the airline provides scheduled and charter domestic and international passenger, VIP and cargo services and utility work with a fleet of three IL-76T/TDs, three Tu-154B-2s, six Tu-154Ms, 11 Yak-40s, 13 Ka-32s, six Mi-8Ts, one Mi-8PS-9 and three Mi-8MTV-1s. Among other things, it provides services to the UN.

Tu-154B-2 RA-85588 (c/n 81A588) lines up for take-off from Moscow-Domodedovo's runway 32L. It is named *Artyom* after a city in the Russian Far East.

Tu-154M RA-85803 (ex 7O-ACT of the South Yemeni carrier Alyemda, c/n 89A822) is named *Spassk-Dal'niy* after another city in the Russian Far East and was purchased from Arax Airways (with which it had flown as EK-85803) in 2000. Before Arax Airways it had been operated by Krai-Aero as RA-85803. *Both Yuriy Kirsanov*

Yak-40 RA-88223 (c/n 9640950) is very appropriately named *Vladivostok*. It is seen here at Khabarovsk-Novyy in February 2002.
Dmitriy Petrochenko

Volga-Aviaexpress

Volga Airlines [G6/VLA] based at Volgograd-Goomrak was the successor of the North Caucasian CAD/Volgograd UFD/231st Flight, operating five Tu-134As, seven Yak-40s and ten Yak-42Ds. The airline adopted a new corporate identity in 1998, changing its name to Volga Aviaexpress [–/WLG]. The airline flies scheduled passenger services in the CIS, plus charters abroad. Here, Tu-134A-3 RA-65903 (c/n (13)63750, f/n 6205), a onetime Tu-134A-3 'Salon' VIP aircraft and one of two remaining in service, is refuelled at Moscow-Domodedovo on 25th November 1998. Note the airport security car which carted this author about the place.
Dmitriy Komissarov

One of the carrier's four Yak-42Ds, RA-42406 (c/n 4520424116683, f/n 0714) was painted in this striking all-blue star-spangled livery in 1998 after an overhaul. Shortly afterwards it was leased to the Rotor football club based in Volgograd. It is seen here landing at Moscow-Domodedovo; the white Volga Aviaexpress titles are almost invisible on the pale blue nose. *Yuriy Kirsanov*

Volga-Dnepr

Volga-Dnepr was the first civil operator of the An-124 which is its main aircraft type. Here, An-124-100 RA-82043 (c/n 9773054155101, f/n 06-07), the second aircraft delivered (as CCCP-82043), taxies in after landing on runway 24 at Moscow-Vnukovo past the hangars of the Vnukovo Aircraft Repair Plant (VARZ). The aircraft wears the additional markings of UK outsize cargo carrier Heavy Lift with which Volga-Dnepr had a partnership until 1st February 2002. *Yuriy Kirsanov*

Volga-Dnepr's first IL-76, RA-76758 (c/n 0073464203, f/n 5601) is seen here at Ul'yanovsk-Vostochnyy. Originally an IL-76TD 'Falsie', it was converted to a 'true' IL-76TD after 1999. Unfortunately it was destroyed by a hurricane at Guam on 8th December 2002. *Volga-Dnepr*

Volga-Dnepr Airlines [VI/VDA] were established in 1990 as the first non-Aeroflot specialised cargo carrier in the USSR/Russia, starting operations in October 1991. It is a joint-stock company with the Antonov Design Bureau, Aviastar and Motor-Sich as the main stockholders. These are respectively the designer, the airframer and the powerplant manufacturer of the airline's main type, the An-124.

Operating from Ul'yanovsk-Vostochnyy, Volga-Dnepr flies scheduled cargo services to Moscow, Novosibirsk, Shenyang and

Tianjin, plus cargo charters all over the world, carrying unique and outsize cargoes. Additionally, the airline operates passenger charters on a small scale. The current fleet consists of nine An-124-100s, with a tenth (an An-124-100M) on order, two IL-76TDs and five Yak-40s. Additionally, Volga-Dnepr has ordered two Boeing 747 freighters.

IL-76TD RA-76798 awaits overhaul at Moscow-Bykovo on on 16th June 2000 after return to Samara Airlines after lease. *Dmitriy Komissarov*

Volga-Dnepr not only carries cargo but performs passenger services as well with a number of Yak-40s. One of them, RA-87357 (c/n 9340631), had this non-standard colour scheme with three-tone blue trim. *Yuriy Kirsanov*

Most of the airline's Yak-40s, including Yak-40K RA-88243 (a former Chelal aircraft) depicted here at Moscow/Vnukovo-1 on 6th May 2003, wear the stylish blue/white standard livery. *Dmitriy Komissarov*

Yak-40 RA-87981 (c/n 9540444) was bought from Simbirsk-Aero in 2001. It is seen here at Moscow/Vnukovo-1 on 5th September 2001 in an all-white colour scheme. *Dmitriy Komissarov*

Vologda Air Enterprise

The Vologda Air Enterprise was formed from the Leningrad CAD/Vologda UAD based at Vologda-Grishino. The enterprise performs scheduled domestic passenger services with eleven Yak-40s of the former 385th Flight and a solitary An-28; it also performs various utility work with 15 An-2s, 15 Mi-2s and three Mi-8Ts. Here, Yak-40 RA-87665 (c/n 9240925) is seen parked at Moscow/Vnukovo-1 on 18th June 2002; it was apparently sold soon afterwards. *Dmitriy Komissarov*

Yak-Service

Yak Service Airline [–/AKY] started operations on 25th November 1993 as the 'house airline' of the Yakovlev Design Bureau, operating business charters from Zhukovskiy and Moscow/Vnukovo-1. The current fleet includes two Yak-40 'Salons 2nd Class', both of which are aircraft reimported from Poland, and two Yak-42Ds in VIP configuration, one of which is operated from IFK-Jets (ie, the Ilyushin Finance Co. leasing company).

Yak-40 'Salon 2nd Class' RA-88295 (ex Polish Air Force '035 red', c/n 9331329) was operated in this colour scheme until at least June 2000. It is seen here at Moscow/Vnukovo-1 on 29th May that year. *Dmitriy Komissarov*

By October 2000 RA-88295 had gained this new and more stylish colour scheme. *Yuriy Kirsanov*

The other Yak-40 'Salon 2nd Class' belonging to Yak Service is RA-88294 (ex Polish Air Force '031 red', c/n 9331029) which was previously operated by Elbrus-Avia and before that by the Petronord petroleum company. It is seen here at Moscow/Vnukovo-1 on 6th May 2003 in the smart livery in which it is operated for a company called ILAN-L since at least March 2002. The Cyrillic logo on the tail (ИЛАН–Л) has been misinterpreted by foreigners as 'Ilana' or even 'Ilavia'. *Dmitriy Komissarov*

Yakutia Airlines

Yakutia Airlines [K7/SYL] were formed in Yakutsk in December 2002, taking over from the Yakutsk Air Enterprise of Sakha Avia. Like its precursor, Yakutia performs scheduled and charter passenger and cargo services. The fleet consists of three An-12s, six An-24RVs, three An-26s, three Tu-154B-2s, five Tu-154Ms and four Yak-40s. One of the Tu-154Ms, RA-85794 (c/n 93A978), displays the airline's appealing livery on approach to Moscow-Sheremet'yevo. *Yuriy Kirsanov*

At least one of Yakutia Airlines' An-26s, RA-26660 (c/n 97308008), has been converted to An-26-100 standard – a convertible passenger/cargo version identifiable by a larger-than-usual number of cabin windows and emergency exits, some of which are discernible in this view. It is seen here in the static park of the MAKS-2003 airshow in Zhukovskiy. *Dmitriy Komissarov*

Yakutsk Airlines

Yakutsk Airlines [–/KUT] were formed in 1999, initially operating a single Tu-154M (RA-85712) leased from Sakha Avia in an all-grey colour scheme with a blue cheatline and appropriate titles and logo representing a stylised snowflake. A second example obtained from the same source – RA-85794 depicted here – was added to the fleet by March 2002, operating in basic Aeroflot colours, along with a single An-24. In December 2002 Yakutsk Airlines merged into the newly-formed Yakutia Airlines (see previous page) and the aircraft were duly repainted.

Yamal Airlines

In early 2000 Yamal Airlines leased Tu-154M RA-85630 (c/n 87A759) from the Rossiya State Transport Co. Here the aircraft is seen parked at the south end of the apron at Moscow/Vnukovo-1 on 29th May 2000; by 4th October it had not moved from the spot. This aircraft is now operated by Kolavia in basic Yamal colours.
Dmitriy Komissarov

Established in 1997, Yamal Airlines [YL/LLM] operate from Salekhard on the Yamal Peninsula in the Russian High North, performing scheduled domestic passenger and cargo flights. The current fleet comprises two An-24RVs, three An-74-200s, two Tu-134As, six Tu-134AKs, two Tu-154B-2s, one Tu-154M, 19 Mi-8Ts and one Mi-8PS-7. The three freighters and one of the Tu-134AKs have been leased to Alliance Avia (see page 16).

Tu-134AK RA-65914 (c/n (33)66109, f/n 6337) vacates Moscow-Sheremet'yevo's runway 25L, turning right towards the Sheremet'yevo-1 terminal after arriving from Salekhard on 26th February 2002.
Dmitriy Komissarov

The Ones that Didn't Make it

Aerofreight Airlines

Moscow-based Aerofreight Airlines (aka Aerofrakht) [–/FRT] founded in 1998 operated seven An-12s, three IL-62Ms, one Tu-154B-2 and two Tu-204-100Cs. The airline's operating licence was cancelled on 2nd September 2003 after one of the aircraft was found to be overloaded by 50%! Pictured above is An-12B. RA-48984 (ex Ukraine Air Alliance UR-48984, c/n 402913); on the left is ex-Aeroflot IL-62M RA-86531 *Ivan* (c/n 4242654) in full red colours at Moscow/Vnukovo-1 on 18th June 2002. Both now serve with **Vim Airlines.** *Above, Dmitriy Petrochenko; Left, Dmitriy Komissarov*

Aerolit

Aerolit (ie, aerolith – an archaic word for meteorite) was a cargo carrier established in1992, operating five An-32 freighters with the non-standard registrations RA-26222 through RA-26225. (That's no way to name an airline, if you don't expect its aircraft to start dropping like stones; as a line from a Russian song goes, 'as you name the yacht, so shall it sail'!) Here, RA-26222 (c/n 2301) is seen at Moscow-Tushino, where it was based together with RA-26223, in 1993. This aircraft was sold to Moscow Airways in 1994 – see page 141. *Yefim Gordon*

Aerotex

Founded in 1997 and based at Moscow/Sheremet'yevo-1, Aerotex flew business charters in the CIS and Western Europe with a fleet of six Yak-40s, a Tu-134AK and a Tu-134A 'Salon'. The airline's licence was withdrawn in the wake of a much-publicised crash of Yak-40D RA-88170 at Moscow-Sheremet'yevo on 9th March 2000 in which the celebrated Russian TV journalist Artyom Borovik was killed.

Yak-40 RA-87440 (c/n 9431635) at Moscow/Vnukovo-1 on 22nd March 2001; most Aerotex aircraft wore this basic ex-Trans Charter livery. Artyom Borovik was to have flown in this aircraft on the fateful day of 9th March 2000. By February 2002 RA-87440 had been sold to Bylina (see page 38). *Dmitriy Komissarov*

In 1999 Aerotex leased Tu-134AK RA-65934 (c/n (33)66143, f/n 6342) from Irkut-Avia, the flying division of the Irkutsk aircraft factory (IAPO). The aircraft retained the eye-catching Irkut-Avia livery, save that the ИРКУТ (IRKUT) titles on the forward fuselage were removed and the IAPO logo replaced by the Aerotex logo. This is one of the three known Tu-134AKs with no galley window or white 'plug' in the first full-size window to starboard. It is now operated by RusLine, as is most of the former Aerotex fleet. *Yuriy Kirsanov*

AJT Air International

Established in 1991, charter carrier AJT Air International (Asia Joint Transport) [E9/TRJ] was one of the first airlines to challenge the monopoly of Aeroflot. Operations were started from Moscow/Vnukovo-1 in 1992., later moving to Sheremet'yevo-1 and -2) Apart from scheduled domestic services to the eastern regions of Russia, the airline flew charters to Western Europe, the Middle East, North Africa and SE Asia with seven IL-86 widebodies and three Tu-154M. The airline's operating licence was withdrawn on 1st September 2003.

Previous page, bottom: IL-86 RA-86140 (c/n 51483211102) in full AJT Air International colours is pushed back at Moscow/Sheremet'yevo-2 on 18th September 1998 before a flight to Hurghada, displaying additional 'Shest' let' titles to mark six years of the airline's existence. *Dmitriy Komissarov*

Above: Leased from Aeroflot Russian International Airlines, IL-86 RA-86065 (c/n 51483204032) was repainted in AJT Air International markings between 30th June and 3rd July 1998, retaining basic ARIA colours; it is seen here at Sheremet'yevo-2 on 11th June 1999. Both aircraft now belong to VASO Airlines. *Dmitriy Komissarov*

ALAK

The charter carrier ALAK [J4/LSV] founded in 1992 and based at Moscow-Vnukovo operated two IL-76TDs, one IL-76MD and three Tu-154Ms until it suspended operations in 1998. The name stands for *aktsionernaya lizingovaya aviakompahniya* (joint-stock leasing airline), since all of the airline's fleet was operated on a lease basis.

Tu-154M RA-85712 (c/n 91A889) seen on approach to Moscow-Vnukovo. RA-85712 was painted identically, while RA-85714 had a red cheatline. The depicted aircraft was sold to Georgian Airlines as 4L-85713. *Yuriy Kirsanov*

IL-76TD RA-76814 (c/n 1013408269, f/n 8208) is seen on short finals to Moscow-Vnukovo, displaying the ALAK tail logo but not the titles which have been scrubbed out (apparently due to a sub-lease). After the airline's demise the aircraft was returned to Rusaeroleasing company from which it had been leased, serving on with a succession of other operators. *Yuriy Kirsanov*

Ashab Air

Ashab Air [–/HAB] – or really Askhab Air (Askhab was a brother-in-arms of the Prophet Muhammad) – was established in 1997 after the First Chechen War as Chechnya's second national airline, purchasing Tu-134A RA-65124 (ex Estonian Air ES-AAN, c/n (83)60560, f/n 4705) in February 1997. Tu-134AK RA-65939 configured as a 72-seater was also leased in 1997-98 in basic Aeroflot colours without titles. The airline's activities were suspended with the outbreak of the Second Chechen War in September 1999; RA-65124 was impounded and has been stored at Zhukovskiy ever since. *Yuriy Kirsanov*

Aviaobshchemash

Founded in 1992, Troitsk-based cargo carrier Aviaobshchemash [–/OBM], also referred to as AOM Air Company, operated a constantly shifting number of aircraft, including at least nine An-12s (ex-Baikal Airlines An-12BP RA-11032 (c/n 7345004) is shown here), An-26s and a single Tu-134AK. As the name implies, the carrier was the flying division of the former Ministry of General Machinery (Minobshchchemash) responsible for the missile and space programmes. The airline's certificate was withdrawn on 2nd December 2003. *Yuriy Kirsanov*

Baikal Airlines

Originally, like many of Russia's new air carriers, Baikal Airlines made minimum changes to the 1973-standard Aeroflot livery, adding only the appropriate titles and tail art representing a gull over the waters of Lake Baikal, as exemplified by Tu-154M RA-85652 (c/n 89A794). Turn back to page 101 to see how this aircraft looks today. *Yuriy Kirsanov*

Later, Baikal Airlines introduced this stylish livery with a basically blue fuselage. On Soviet-built aircraft the belly was still grey, as illustrated by Tu-154B-2 RA-85453 (c/n 80A453) seen on approach to Moscow-Domodedovo. This aircraft is now operated by Sibir', still in basic Baikal Airlines colours. *Yuriy Kirsanov*

Baikal Airlines was the second Russian operator of the Boeing 757 (after Transaero), leasing Boeing 757-2Q8 N321LF (c/n 26269, f/n 612) from ILFC in 1995; this was the first aircraft to wear the carrier's new livery. The airliner was returned in 1996 when the Russian customs authorities demanded that import duties be paid; it later went to Avianca Colombia. *Yuriy Kirsanov*

Baikal Airlines (Baikalavia) [X3/BKL] was the successor of the East Siberian CAD/Irkutsk UAD comprising the 134th Flight (operating An-12s, An-24 and IL-76s), the 190th Flight (operating An-2s and An-26s), the 201st Flight (operating Tu-154s) and a further Flight operating Mi-8s. The carrier performed domestic and international sched-uled passenger services and cargo charters with four An-2s, six An-12B/BPs, eight An-24RVs, six An-26s, four IL-76Ts, two IL-76TDs, five Tu-154B-2s, five Tu-154Ms, five Mi-8Ts, one Mi-8PS and two Mi-8MTV-1s.

The airline's financial position was shaky in the late 1990s and plans of a merger with Chitaavia in the hope of improving things were announced in April 1998. However, the 1998 bank crisis ruined these plans and Baikal Airlines filed for bankruptcy in September. Operations were restarted on a small scale under outside management in the spring of 1999 but the company finally vanished soon afterwards.

Some of Baikal Airlines' An-24RVs also wore full colours, as illustrated by rather faded-looking RA-46629 (c/n 37308808) stored at Irkutsk-1. *Dmitriy Petrochenko*

Chernomor-Soyuz

Chernomor Soyuz [–/CHZ], a charter airline based in the Black sea resort city of Sochi (the name translates loosely as Black Sea Union) was founded in 1995, flew passenger charters with two ex-East German Tu-134s (a Tu-134AK and a Tu-134A) and a pair of Tu-154B-1s. The airline ceased operations in 1998.

Tu-134A RA-65605 (ex Belair EW-65605, ex CCCP-65605 No. 2, ex-D-AOBI, ex-DDR-SCU; c/n (43)09070, f/n 2310) applies reverse thrust after landing on runway 06 at Moscow-Vnukovo. The aircraft retains the faded basic livery of previous operator Chernomorskie Airlines (= Black Sea Airlines, hence the 'surf' on the cheatline) with Chernomor Soyuz titles in English. *Yuriy Kirsanov*

The same aircraft at a later date, following overhaul and repair in basic Aeroflot colours with Cyrillic titles. Originally bought by Komiavia, CCCP-65605 No. 2 was sold to the Minsk aircraft overhaul plant to pay for the refurbishment of other aircraft and has been changing hands ever since. *Yuriy Kirsanov*

Diamond Sakha

Established in 1993, Diamond Sakha Airlines based at Neryungri-Chool'man was Russia's second operator of the Airbus A310, receiving two former Pan American A310-324(ET)s – N820PA and N821PA (c/ns 457 and 458) – in June and July 1995. The aircraft were placed on the French overseas register as F-OGYM and F-OGYN respectively, gaining this striking livery reflecting the diamond-rich status of the Republic of Yakutia (Sakha). Both aircraft were operated jointly with Aeroflot Russian International Airlines, as indicated by the tiny Aeroflot titles under the foremost doors. Both machines were transferred to another Yakutian air carrier called Savial – Sakha Airlines (not to be confused with Sakha Avia) in 1998. *Dmitriy Petrochenko*

Etele Air

Etele Air [–/ETO] founded in 1996 flew passenger and cargo charters with a single Yak-40 'Salon' and two An-12Bs. The airline's operating licence was cancelled in 2003. Here, civil-configured An-12B RA-11117 (c/n 5402707) comes in to land at Moscow-Domodedovo. The aircraft retains the basic colours of the defunct Aviacor (the flying division of the Samara aircraft factory) from which it was bought in 1998. After the demise of Etele Air RA-11117 was sold to a Ukrainian airline as UR-CBZ. *Yuriy Kirsanov*

Eurasia Airlines

Eurasia Airlines [UH/EUS] started life in 1997. In 2001 the airline moved from Moscow-Bykovo to Vnukovo-1, operating scheduled and charter services with two Yak-40s, two Tu-154B-2s, one Tu-154M, an IL-86 and two An-12s. In 2003, however, the GSGA unearthed advanced corrosion on one aircraft (Tu-154B-2 RA-85467) and withdrew Eurasia's licence on 17th September 2003.

Pictured at Moscow/Vnukovo-1 on 18th June 2002, Yak-40K RA-88247 (c/n 9642051) gained Eurasia Airlines colours after return from lease to Iranian charter carrier Kish Air as EP-LBJ. This aircraft had Russian titles on both sides. Eurasia's other Yak-40 (RA-88171, formerly leased to Kish Air as EP-LBK) had a white/grey scheme with no markings. *Dmitriy Komissarov*

Eurasia Airlines used their sole IL-86 RA-86125 (c/n 51483210093) as a 'flying billboard'. It is seen at Moscow/Vnukovo-1 on the same day as a large R&K Computers logo was removed from the fuselage. In November 2003 this aircraft was already operated by Atlant-Soyuz in Eurasia Airlines colours. *Dmitriy Komissarov*

IRS Aero

Established in 1997, IRS Aero [LD/LDF, later 5R/LDF] operated passenger and cargo charters from Moscow-Sheremet'yevo and Zhukovskiy with a mix of own and leased aircraft, including two Tu-154s. Here, Tu-154B-2 RA-85333 (c/n 79A333) leased from the State Civil Aviation Research Institute (GosNII GA), comes in to land at Moscow-Sheremet'yevo; the other example was Tu-154M RA-85696 leased from Mavial. *Yuriy Kirsanov*

The largest aircraft operated by IRS Aero was IL-86 RA-86136 (c/n 51483210094). After the demise of IRS Aero the aircraft was stripped of all titles and operated by Continental Airways in an anonymous all-white scheme. *S. and D. Komissarov collection*

The IL-18 was the first aircraft operated by IRS Aero, four of these being operated in combi and freighter configurations. IL-18V RA-75840 (c/n 182005301) bought on 2nd October 1998 is a former IL-18RT flying telemetry relay station used during missile tests, as revealed by the non-standard fat tailcone where a 'thimble' radome used to be. It is seen here taking off from runway 12 at Zhukovskiy on 13th August 2001. Just over three months later, on 19th November, the aircraft crashed near Kalyazin, Russia, killing all 27 occupants. Yet it was not this crash but the discovery of several grave breaches (mostly forged paperwork) which eventually led the Russian CAA to withdraw IRS Aero's operating licence in late 2002. *Dmitriy Komissarov*

Korsar

Established in 1991, Korsar [6K/KRS] flew business and cargo charters from Moscow/Vnukovo-3, mostly with aircraft leased from such operators as the government flight (the 235th Independent Air Detachment), Aeroflot and the NPO Energiya aerospace industry corporation. Korsar is Russian for 'corsair', but the name had nothing to do with pirates; it derives from the names of the airline's founders, Korovin and Sarzhveladze. Here, one of the airline's Tu-134AKs, RA-65719 (c/n (13)63637, f/n 6106) is seen at Moscow/Vnukovo-3 on 14th June 1996; this aircraft and Yak-40K RA-88298 were the only ones to wear full Korsar livery. The airline also operated such types as the An-12, An-26, IL-76TD and Tu-154M. Korsar ceased operations in 1997. *Dmitriy Komissarov*

Kumertau Express

Kumertau Express (later Kumertau Airlines) was the flying division of the Kumertau Aircraft Production Enterprise (KumAPP) in Bashkiria, a manufacturer of Kamov helicopters. Over the years it operated single examples of the An-8, An-12B, An-30, Tu-134A 'Salon' and Yak-40. Here, An-30A RA-46632 (c/n 0201), the first production example, is seen in full company colours at Moscow-Bykovo on 25th September 1999. The airline suspended operations in 2001. *Dmitriy Komissarov*

Magadanaerogrooz

Magadanaerogrooz (= Magadan Air Cargo, or Magadan Cargo Airlines) [–/MGG] operated scheduled and charter cargo services with seven An-12s and three IL-76TDs until it went out of business in 1998. Here, civil-configured An-12BP RA-12984 (c/n 00347109) is pictured in brilliant sunshine at Moscow-Domodedovo on 20th November 1998. Note that the registration is carried on the fin fillet instead of the fuselage as is customary; this is because the Ivchenko AI-20 turboprops are extremely smoky and the rear fuselage soon gets covered in soot, making the registration illegible.
Dmitriy Komissarov

Close-up of the forward fuselage of RA-12984, showing the МАГ (MAG = Magadanaerogrooz) badge and 'Cargo Service' titles. Traces of the titles of a former operator called The (!) Atlantic Airlines are still discernible above the windows. The aircraft was later sold to Magadanavialeasing.
Dmitriy Komissarov

Moscow Airways

Established in 1991 and based at Sheremet'yevo-2, Moscow Airways (aka *Moskovskiye avialinii*) [M8/MSC] owned this IL-76TD, RA-76498 (c/n 0023442218, f/n 3105); it is pictured here on the cargo apron at its home base. By early 1995 it was joined by another example (RA-76355) leased from the Beriyev Design Bureau in all-white colours. After the demise of Moscow Airways RA-76498 (which was one of only two aircraft painted in full airline colours) was sold to Continental Airways (see page 40). *Yuriy Kirsanov*

Moscow Airways also operated scheduled and charter cargo flights with two Tu-154s (a 'B-2 and an 'M) leased from the Tupolev Design Bureau and with two IL-62Ms, one of which was this standard example (RA-86507, c/n 2035546) leased from the Ul'yanovsk Civil Aviation School in 1993-94. The other aircraft (RA-86515) was an IL-62M 'Salon TM-3SUR' painted in full colours with a grey top; stripped of its VIP interior and being a former navigation systems testbed, it retained the characteristic fat spine associated with satellite communications gear. *Yuriy Kirsanov*

Moscow Airways operated three An-32 freighters, including An-32B RA-26222 (c/n 2301) – a converted An-32 *sans suffixe* bought from Aerolit in 1994. It was the crash of this aircraft at Kinshasa-N'dolo on 8th January 1996 when the overloaded freighter failed to become airborne and ploughed through the adjacent Simba Zikita market, killing some 260 people, that led to Moscow Airways' licence being revoked. *Yuriy Kirsanov*

Mostransgaz

Mostransgaz, one of the Russian natural gas industry's many flying divisions, operated a single An-12TB, a single IL-76TD, a Tu-134AK and two former CSA Czech Airlines Yak-40s converted to VIP configuration, as well as a numerous Ka-26 utility choppers and a Mi-8PS VIP helicopter. A Bell 206L-3 LongRanger was also ordered but never delivered. In April 1997 the airline was integrated into Gazpromavia (which see). Here, Yak-40 'Salon 2nd Class' RA-88306 (ex OK-GEL, c/n 9640651) is seen in Mostransgaz livery at Ostaf'yevo; note the dorsal satcom blister. *Mike Kell*

Murmansk Airlines

Murmansk Airlines (Murmanskiye Avialinii) [–/MNK] was formed from the Leningrad CAD/Murmansk UAD based at Murmashi airport, operating six An-2s, four Tu-154Ms, nine Ka-32S/Ts, 13 Mi-2s and five Mi-8s. The 1998 crisis proved insurmountable for the carrier and the airline was put up for sale. Eventually no buyer could be found and the airline wound down in 1999, the serviceable aircraft being sold off piecemeal. Here, Tu-154M RA-85799 (c/n 94A983), which, like the other three, flew in Russian Aviation Consortium colours, is seen on finals to Moscow-Vnukovo's runway 24 in September 1998. *Dmitriy Komissarov*

Orient Avia

Moscow/Sheremet'yevo-1 based Orient Avia [V6/ORT] flew scheduled passenger services, mostly to the Russian Far East (hence the name), and charters abroad with a fleet of four IL-62Ms and one IL-86. Wishing to expand its route network, the airline bought a pair of Tu-134A-3s in 1996. However, Orient Avia suffered serious financial troubles. In an attempt to resolve them the carrier approached East Line (then a pure cargo airline), trying to negotiate a merger. Yet the deal fell through and on 10th July 1997 Orient Avia filed for bankruptcy. Here, the sole IL-86 in the fleet, RA-86115 (c/n 51483209083) named *Antalya* is seen in the airline's attractive livery in 1996; it was sold to AJT Air International in 1997. *Yuriy Kirsanov*

IL-62M RA-86567 *Primor'ye* (c/n 4256314) is pictured on approach to Moscow-Sheremet'yevo. After sitting in storage at this airport for nearly two years the aircraft was made operational again and sold to East Line. RA-86568 *Vladivostok* and RA-86126 *Kazan'* were painted identically, whereas RA-86590 *Nakhodka* (ex Ensor Air OK-BYZ) wore a blue shade instead of the usual emerald green. *Yuriy Kirsanov*

Oryol Avia

Often referred to in Western publications as 'Orel Avia', Oryol Avia [–/UVL] was not based in Oryol (contrary to its name) but in Lipetsk, operating three Yak-40s and five Yak-42Ds, including RA-42422 (c/n 4520424304017) seen here; three Tu-204s were ordered but never delivered. 'Oryol' is Russian for 'eagle', which explains the mischievously grinning eagle on the tail. Oryol Avia merged into Vnukovo Airlines in 1998. *Yuriy Kirsanov*

Permtransavia-PM

Perm'transavia-PM [–/PMT], the flying division of the Perm' Engine Factory (hence the PM for *Permskiye motory*), operated an An-26B, a Tu-134K (RA-65669, the last 'short' Tu-134 to remain operational), a Tu-134AK, a Yak-40 and a Mi-8. Tu-134AK RA-65983, a former Russian Air Force Tu-134 Balkany (c/n (03)63350, f/n 5808) bought in February 1997, is seen here; it was the only aircraft to wear the airline's full colours. The airline vanished in 1998, RA-65983 being sold to Gazpromavia in April of that year. *Yuriy Kirsanov*

Ramair

Ramair [–/RMY], a cargo charter operator based at Chelyabinsk (Russia) and Sharjah (UAE), operated four IL-18s.

A former special mission aircraft operated by GosNII GA, IL-18D RA-75442 (c/n 187009702) 'cleans up' after a characteristically smoky take-off, displaying Ramair's full livery. Only the blister above the flight deck left over from a star tracker identifies it as the former one-of-a-kind IL-18D 'Tsiklon' weather research aircraft. RA-75442 was leased from GosNII GA from 20th July 1997 to 31st December 1998 and eventually sold to Phoenix Aviation as EX-75442 in Ramair colours. *Yuriy Kirsanov*

IL-18D RA-75466 *Nadym* (c/n 187010403), a former IL-24N long-range ice reconnaissance aircraft bought from GosNII GA in July 1997, takes off, displaying its Domodedovo CAPA-style cheatline with a red pinstripe and the all-blue tail. The aircraft was sold to an unknown operator in November 1998. *Yuriy Kirsanov*

RDS-Avia

RDS-Avia, an obscure operator based at Ostaf'yevo, was the flying division of the RDS (*Roosskiy Dom Selenga* – Selenga Russian House) trading company which eventually turned out to be a front for a wide-scale scam (a financial pyramid). The only known aircraft it operated was An-74-200 RA-74045 (c/n 365.470.97.938, f/n 1608). Here the aircraft is shown at its home base in 2002, still wearing the RDS-Avia badge after the company had vanished.

Mike Kell

Remex

Moscow-based charter carrier Remex [–/RXM] operated mostly cargo charters from Zhukovskiy with five IL-76s. The airline ceased operations in late 2000.

The first freighter operated by Remex, IL-76TD RA-76354 (c/n 1013409280, f/n 8210) takes off from runway 14L at Moscow-Domodedovo in 1998. The red-underlined cheatline is that of Aviakompaniya Ural (from which it was leased), not the Domodedovo CAPA. In November 1998 the aircraft was returned and sold to AZAL Avia Cargo as 4K-AZ11.
Yuriy Kirsanov

Remex also tried operating passenger charters for a while. Here, all-white Yak-42D RA-42325 (c/n 4520424402148, f/n 0306) leased from Saravia takes off from Moscow-Vnukovo's runway 24 in 1998, showing small Remex titles on the nose.
Yuriy Kotel'nikov

Roos' JSC

Roos' Air Transport Company [–/RUR] (Roos' is an old-style poetic name of Russia) was founded in November 1999 as a cargo carrier, operating five IL-76TDs, three of which were converted from IL-76MDs, and a single IL-76T. In 2000 the airline moved into the passenger charter market with a single leased Tu-154M (RA-85766). On 6th December 2000 Roos' bought Tu-134A-1 4L-AAE from former Georgian flag carrier ORBI. However, before the latter aircraft had a chance to be refurbished and reregistered, IL-76TD RA-76588 crashed fatally on take-off from Chkalovskaya AB on 14th July 2001 due to overloading and pilot error. The ensuing investigation resulted in the airline's operating licence being withdrawn. Here, RA-76591 (c/n 0043452546, f/n 3907), the airline's first aircraft, completes its landing run at Moscow-Vnukovo. *Yuriy Kirsanov*

Severaero

Severaero (= Northaero) [–/NOT] based at Noril'sk-Alykel' in the Krasnoyarsk Region briefly operated Tu-134A RA-65605 and Tu-154B-2 RA-85504 in 1998 but ceased operations in 1999. The latter aircraft is depicted here at Moscow-Domodedovo on 20th September 1998 shortly before sale to Omskavia (see page 80).

Dmitriy Komissarov

SPAir

SPAIR Air Transport Corporation [–/PAR] (*Aviatrahnsportnaya korporahtsiya Spaer*) based at Yekaterinburg-Kol'tsovo was mainly concerned with cargo carriage, operating four An-12s and four IL-76T/MDs. The letters SP in the carrier's name were derived from the name of its director, Valeriy Spoornov. Here, one of the airline's An-12BPs, RA-11049 (c/n 8346109), is seen landing at Moscow-Domodedovo – possibly after the airline's demise in 1999 and the aircraft's sale to the Yermolino Flight Test & Research Enterprise, as the aircraft carries SPAIR logos but no titles. Note that the aircraft has been demilitarised. *Yuriy Kirsanov*

In 1996-98 SPAIR leased Tu-154B-2 RA-85312 (c/n 78A312) from Perm Airlines, making the appropriate alterations to the basic Aeroflot livery. The aircraft is seen here completing its landing run on Moscow-Domodedovo's runway 32L, with the huge maintenance hangar in the background. Additionally, SPAIR briefly leased Tu-134A-3 RA-65786 from Chelal in September 1994. *Yuriy Kirsanov*

Special Cargo Airlines

Special Cargo Airlines (*Spetsiahl'nyye groozovyye avialinii*) [C7/SCI] founded in 1991 and based at Yermolino south of Moscow operated seven An-2s, ten An-12B/BPs, three An-26s and one Mi-8. Although it has a small radome, demilitarised RA-11329 (ex CCCP-11329 No. 2, c/n 8346010) is reportedly a converted An-12BK which has had the Initsiativa-4-100 radar replaced with an ROZ-1 radar after being disposed of by the Soviet Air Force. This aircraft was sold to the Angolan airline Hellier International in 1998 as D2-FBZ.The airline suspended operations in 2000. *Yuriy Kirsanov*

Start

Start Air Transport Co. based in Zhukovskiy had a single An-12BK, RA-13331 (ex Soviet Air Force '10 Red', ex CCCP-48974, c/n 6344510) bought from the Flight Research Institute in 1994. This was a highly non-standard aircraft retaining traces of earlier use as a de-icing systems testbed (two large observation blisters on the upper forward fuselage sides for filming the dorsally mounted test article). Interestingly, the titles were an attempt to combine the Roman (START) and Cyrillic (CTAPT) rendering, and the result was something in between (CSTART). Here the aircraft is seen carrying additional Interaviatrans titles. *Yuriy Kirsanov*

Tatneft'aero Inc. [–/TNF] was formed in 2000 as the airline of the Tatneft' (Tatarstan Oil Co.) corporation, operating scheduled and charters services with two Tu-154Ms (RA-85798 and RA-85799) from Kazan'-Osnovnoy. A radar-nosed Tu-134AK was added to the fleet in January 2001; additionally, Tatneft' operated two Yak-40 'Salons 2nd Class'. In February 2002 Tatneft'aero suspended operations and the aircraft were sold off. Here RA-85798 (c/n 94A982) is seen at Moscow/Vnukovo-1 on 4th October 2000.
Dmitriy Komissarov

Dmitriy Komissarov

Stela

Based in Irkutsk, Stela was one of the first post-Soviet specialised air freight carriers, operating two An-32Bs in this pleasing colour scheme. Here, An-32B 48071 (c/n 2909) is pictured in the static park of MosAeroShow-92 (11th-16th August). The aircraft carries no nationality prefix because the RA- prefix was not officially adopted yet, variations such as RF-, РФ- and РОССИЯ- being in use.

Touch & Go/Konveyer

In 1993 the Moscow airline Konveyer [EC/TUG], a passenger and cargo charter carrier, leased an IL-76TD from Mostransgaz and this Tu-154M (RA-85756) from Daghestan Airlines. Generally *konveyer* means 'conveyor belt' or 'assembly line' in Russian; as an aviation term, however, it means 'touch and go', hence the airline's other name, Touch & Go Ltd. The airline vanished by 1996, the two aircraft returning to their respective owners. *Yuriy Kirsanov*

Transaero Express

Business charter operator Transaero Express [–/TXE] was formed in 1994 as a sister company of Transaero, operating a succession of three Tu-134s and two Yak-40 'Salons 2nd Class' from Moscow/Sheremet'yevo-1. The airline suspended operations in 2002. Each of Transaero Express's aircraft had a different livery. Thus, Tu-134AK RA-65830 (c/n (43)12093, f/n 2409) depicted on this page wore a red/blue cheatline and tail stripes, plus large Transaero Express titles. It was sold to Karat in July 1999. Tu-134AK RA-65926 (c/n (33)66101, f/n 6336) on the opposite page wore the full colours of Volare from which it was leased in 1995 with the addition of Transaero Express titles.

Both photos, Yuriy Kirsanov

Transaero Samara

Cargo carrier Trans Aero Samara [–/TSL] based at Samara-Bezymyanka had two An-12s and two IL-76TDs, including RA-76381 (c/n 1033418596, f/n 9009) seen here becoming airborne from Moscow-Domodedovo's runway 32L. Despite the similar name, this airline had nothing to do with Transaero. In 1999 the airline ceased operations, selling both IL-76s to East Line. An-12BP RA-11962 was sold to Aviast; the fate of the other An-12 (RA-11363) is unknown. *Yuriy Kirsanov*

Trans-Charter

Founded in February 1994, Moscow-based Trans-Charter [–/TCH] operated cargo and passenger charters with a fleet of two An-124-100s, three IL-76s, two An-32s and this Yak-40 'Salon 2nd Class', RA-87662 (c/n 9240625) pictured at Moscow-Bykovo on 17th March 1996. This aircraft was sold to Dvin-Avia of Armenia by May 1996 as EK-87662. The airline ceased operations in 1999; interestingly, the livery depicted here lived on with another charter carrier, AeroTeks.

Transeuropean Airlines

Transeuropean Airlines was founded in 1996, operating passenger charters abroad with aircraft initially leased from other carriers as required. In 1999 the fleet comprised four Il-86s and ono Tu 154M. The planned purchase of two IL-96-300s never materialised; instead, the carrier bought a brand-new Tu-204-100 in May 1999 and had a second aircraft on order but went out of business that year.

Transeuropean Airlines' first Tu-154M, RA-85676 (c/n 90A836) leased from Khakasia Airlines in 1996 wore basic Aeroflot colours with Transeuropean titles/logo and the registration on the fuselage. *Yuriy Kirsanov*

In contrast, Tu-154M RA-85799 leased from Murmansk Airlines received the stylish full blue/white livery. *Yuriy Kirsanov*

A sight to be seen no more – unfortunately. Tu-204-100 RA-64018 (c/n 1450741964018) looks absolutely magnificent as it taxies out at Moscow/Sheremet'yevo-2 for take-off from runway 07L – probably on 11th June 1999, the day of the type's inaugural service with Transeuropean Airlines – with a landing Aeroflot Russian International Airlines Tu-134AK in the background. Turn to page 74 to see how this aircraft looks today. Note the blue tail of ex-Transeuropean IL-86 RA-86145 right beside the characteristic mushroom concourse of Sheremet'yevo-1 across the field. *Yuriy Kirsanov*

Tret'yakovo Airlines

Acquired in 1999, IL-18D RA-74296 (c/n 188010603) originally flew in Aeroflot colours without titles but later gained full colours. Here it is depicted at Moscow/Vnukovo-1 on 6th May 2002, by which time it had been christened *Moskva*. *Dmitriy Komissarov*

The Tret'yakovo Air Transport Company [–/TKO] started operations in 1997 with An-26s leased as required. Gradually it expanded its fleet to two IL-18s, three IL-62Ms and three Tu-134A/AKs, flying passenger and cargo charters from Moscow-Domodedovo and Lookhovitsy-Tret'yakovo, the factory airfield of the Moscow Aircraft Production Association (MAPO). The airline's certificate was withdrawn on 30th January 2003 after a crash late in the preceding year.

Tu-134A-3 RA-65057 (c/n (73)49865, f/n 3909) was leased from Voronezhavia in 2001, retaining the blue/yellow Voronezhavia cheatline. *Yuriy Kirsanov*

Former Dalavia Far East Airways IL-62M RA-86452 (c/n 1622212) sits under a sullen sky at Moscow/Vnukovo-1 on 18th February 2002. It was the crash of this aircraft on landing at Bishkek-Manas on 23rd October 2002 that resulted in the airline's operating licence being revoked. *Dmitriy Komissarov*

Tyumen' Airlines

Tyumen' Airlines/*Tyumenskiye avialinii* [7M/TYM] based at Tyumen'-Roschchino started life in 1992 as the successor of the Tyumen' CAD/2nd Tyumen' UAD comprising the 259th, 357th and 435th Flights (operating the Tu-134A/Tu-154, An-24/ An-26 and An-12/IL-76 respectively). This was one of the two major air carriers in the Tyumen' Region, operating scheduled domestic and regional passenger services and cargo charters with a fleet consisting lately of one An-12B, six An-24Bs, four IL-76Ts, one IL-76TD, nine Tu-134As and seven Tu-154B-1/B-2s.

However, the airline's financial state went from bad to worse after the 1998 Russian bank crisis and eventually the carrier was declared bankrupt, ceasing operations on 1st November 2003 when no buyer could be found. The fate of the fleet (including the nine surviving Tu-134s) remains to be seen. The licence was cancelled on 5th December 2003

Some Tyumen' Airlines Tu-134As, like RA-65738 (c/n 2351507) leased from the Siberian Aviation Research Institute (SibNIA), had nothing more than a slightly modified Aeroflot livery. The green radome on this one is unusual. *Yuriy Kirsanov*

Seen here just as it touches down on runway 32L at Moscow-Domodedovo, Tu-134A-3 RA-65009 (c/n (63)46120, f/n 3308) exemplifies the full livery. The logo is the stylised blue flame of burning natural gas in which the Tyumen' Region is abundant. *Yuriy Kirsanov*

Wheels caught in mid-retraction, Tyumen' Airlines IL-76TD RA-76807 (c/n 1013405176, f/n 8004) still wears additional 'Jet Air Cargo – Operated by Jet Aviation Business Jets AG, Switzerland' and 'Ilavia' titles dating back to previous leases. *Yuriy Kirsanov*

An-24RV RA-47778 (c/n 79901502), a converted An-24B, shows off full Tyumen' Airlines colours as it taxies for take-off at Tyumen'-Roshchino. *Dmitriy Petrochenko*

Tu-154B-1 RA-85255 (c/n 77A255) in full Tyumen' Airlines livery is seen on final approach to Moscow-Domodedovo. *Yuriy Kirsanov*

Vnukovo Airlines

Established in 1993 as the successor of the Vnukovo Civil Aviation Production Association comprising the 65th and 200th Flights which operated the IL-86 and Tu-154 respectively, Vnukovo Airlines/*Vnookovskiye avialinii* (VA) was Russia's second-largest carrier as regards passenger numbers, ranking second only to ARIA. In 1997 VA was doing fine, joining the Russian Aviation Consortium (a short-lived joint venture with Murmansk Airlines) and swallowing Oryol Avia with its small fleet of Yak-42Ds. Apart from these, the huge fleet included 22 IL-86s, one Tu-154C, three Tu-154B-1s, one Tu-154B-2, 19 Tu-154Ms and three Tu-204s, though many of them were grounded, being high-time airframes.

In the late 1990s, however, the airline began experiencing problems, with frequent changes of the top executives and labour/management conflicts over working conditions. Back in the summer of 1998 Vladislav Filyov, General Director of Sibir' Airlines, stated that Sibir' needed to make a strategic alliance with a major Moscow-based carrier (in order to gain a foothold in the capital), and VA was viewed as the prime candidate.

Negotiations over the alliance (or should we say takeover?) continued for some time but were interrupted when VA ran into financial and labour relations problems. Eventually Sibir' did take over the ailing giant, Vnukovo Airlines suspending operations in late 2001 and most of the airworthy fleet going to Sibir'.

Vnukovo Airlines' Tu-154B/B-1/B-2s never received the carrier's full livery adopted in 1993, flying in Aeroflot colours without titles, as illustrated by Tu-154B RA-85099 (c/n 75A099). *Yuriy Kirsanov*

Tu-154M RA-85743 (c/n 92A926) was likewise never repainted but did gain the appropriate titles after all. In 2001 this aircraft was used in support of the Russian National Soccer Team, as indicated by the badge aft of the flight deck and the legend on the fuselage. *Yuriy Kirsanov*

Tu-154M RA-85736 (c/n 92A918) in Vnukovo Airlines' standard livery touches down on Moscow-Vnukovo's runway 24 as the thrust reversers begin to deploy. This livery has earned the uncomplimentary nickname 'bandaged dick'. Note that the titles are different to port and starboard. *Yuriy Kirsanov*

Above and right: Pinstripes are stylish, aren't they? Three Vnukovo Airlines Tu-154Ms – RA-85615 (c/n 86A731) seen here at Moscow-Domodedovo on 11th November 1998, RA-85619 and RA-85673 – wore Russian Aviation Consortium colours.

Dmitriy Komissarov

Tu-154B-2 RA-85312 retained a SPAIR-like colour scheme long after that airline had vanished. In May 2000 it was leased by Vnukovo Airlines from Perm Airlines; it is depicted here at Anapa-Vityazevo in the summer of 2001. *Yefim Gordon*

RA-86081 (c/n 51483206052) was the only one of Vnukovo Airlines' IL-86s to wear the Russian Aviation Consortium colours. It is seen here lifting off from Moscow-Vnukovo's runway 24 as it passes the intersection with runway 02/20. *Yuriy Kirsanov*

sSeen here on short finals to Moscow-Vnukovo's runway 24 in September 1998, RA-86085 (c/n 51483206056) was probably the first aircraft to be painted in full Vnukovo Airlines colours. *Dmitriy Komissarov*

As the Yak-42Ds taken over over from Oryol Avia had been sold by the spring of 2000, Vnukovo Airlines obtained two further examples to be used instead of Tu-154s and IL-86s, matching the decline in passenger numbers. One was RA-42362 (ex LY-AAX, c/n 4520424811431, f/n 0709) which flew in faded basic 1994-standard orange/grey Lithuanian Airlines livery. The other was RA42446 (the registration was applied with no dash or space; c/n 4520423308017) seen here at Moscow/Vnukovo-1 on 29th May 2000. It was reportedly leased from FAPSI (the now-disbanded Russian Federal Government Communications & Information Agency) in this anonymous colour scheme, featuring a VIP interior and HF special communications equipment whose presence is revealed by the non-standard tandem unswept blade aerials on top of the fin. Both aircraft wore only a small VA logo aft of the flight deck. RA-42362 was sold to Elbrus-Avia in 2001, while RA42441 was transferred to EMERCOM of Russia (the federal civil aid and disaster relief agency) during the same year. *Dmitriy Komissarov*

Being traditionally the first Aeroflot subdivision to receive new hardware, the Vnukovo CAPA had held route-proving trials of the Tu-204; thus Vnukovo Airlines were the first carrier to launch revenue services with the type. Here, Tu-204 (not yet a -100) RA-64011 (c/n 1450741364011) is seen at Moscow-Domodedovo on 3rd November 1998. Yes, Domodedovo. Vnukovo Airlines' financial problems were serious enough to force the carrier to move part of their fleet to Domodedovo where airport charges were lower and fuel was always readily available (unlike Vnukovo). *Dmitriy Komissarov*

Vostsibaero

Founded in 1995, Irkutsk-based Vostsibaero (= East Siberia Air) operated passenger and cargo charters with a single An-26, two An-74s and this Yak-40 'Salon 1st Class', RA-87655 (c/n 9211820), which in Soviet times had been the aircraft of the First Secretary of the Krasnoyarsk Regional Committee of the Communist Party. Vostsibaero's licence was revoked in 1999 after An-74-200 RA-74037 was written off in a non-fatal crash in Mirnyy. Here RA-87655 is shown at Moscow/Vnukovo-1 on 6th May 2003, still wearing Vostsibaero tail colours and Interprobusiness-M Ltd. titles on the nose. *Dmitriy Komissarov*

Voronezhavia

Established on 20th January 1999 as the former Central Regions CAD/Voronezh UAD/243rd Flight, Voronezhavia was one of the largest carriers based in Russia's bread belt. The airline flew scheduled and charter services from Voronezh-Chertovitskoye to various destinations in central, southern and western Russia. It also performed utility, crop-spraying and agricultural/ecological survey work; the unique Tu-134SKh aircraft, of which Voronezhavia was the main operator, were used for this.

The sizeable fleet included 28 An-2 utility aircraft, ten An-24B/RV regional airliners, five Tu-134As, two Tu-134AKs, six Tu-134SKh surveyors and two Yak-42s. Like most Russian regional airlines, Voronezhavia was hard hit by the 1998 crisis which forced the airline to sell off surplus aircraft (first of all the Yak-42s) and lease the remaining to other carriers as required, including business charter operators which had two of the carrier's Tu-134As (RA-65067 and RA-65794) converted to Tu-134A 'Salons' to suit their needs. However, the crunch came when Tu-134SKh RA-65929 – the only one which had 'kept the faith' and had not yet been converted into a Tu-134A-3M – overran the runway at Nyagan', Tyumen' Region, after aborting a take-off at high speed; it was this accident which led the Russian CAA to cancel the airline's operating licence on 30th November.

RA-65929, the last remaining Tu-134SKh (c/n (63)66495, f/n 6373), seen visiting Novosibirsk-Tolmachovo. It retained the characteristic 'ear of wheat' and Cyrillic 'SKh' (CX) markings on the nose after Voronezhavia titles were applied but the mission equipment, including the characteristic pods of the Nit' S-1SKh SLAR, has been removed. *Dmitriy Petrochenko*

VTS-Trans

In 1999 Moscow-based start-up VTS-Trans, a subsidiary of the Vneshtorgservis (= foreign trade service) company, leased Tu-134AK RA-65939 (ex Balkan Bulgarian Airlines LZ-TUU, c/n 1351409) from Gromov Air. The aircraft received an all-new interior designed by the Tupolev Joint-Stock Co. and installed at the company's flight test facility in Zhukovskiy, where the aircraft is pictured on 23rd September. VTS-Trans took delivery of the aircraft on 26th September 1999. In March 2001 RA-65939 was sold to Chernomor-Avia and reverted to 72-seat configuration.

Dmitriy Komissarov

YeLIIP (Yermolino Airlines)

The Yermolino Flight Test & Research Enterprise (YeLIIP – *Yermolinskoye lyotno-ispytahtel'noye issledovatel'skoye predpriyahtiye*) [–/EFE], later renamed Yermolino Airlines, operated seven An-12s and three Tu-134AKsfrom Yermolino. The VIP jets were operated for such enterprises as leasing them to SBS-Bank and the Aviazapchast' spares supply agency. In 2002 Yermolino Airlines ceased operations, most of the fleet being purchased by co-located Antex-Polus. Here, An-12BP RA-11768 (c/n 5343103) catches the last rays of the setting sun at Moscow-Domodedovo on 25th November 1998.

Dmitriy Komissarov

Yukosavia

Yukosavia, the flying division of the Yukos Oil Co. (which recently gained notoriety due to the arrest of oil tycoon Mikhail Khodorkovskiy), operated Tu-134s leased as required. Most were 80-seaters used for carrying shifts of oil workers to airports located close to major oilfields; however, Tu-134AK RA-65606 leased from komiavia in July 1997 (ex CCCP-65606 No. 2, ex Interflug D-AOBR, ex DDR-SDH, c/n (63)46300, f/n 3405) retained its VIP interior. The airline ceased operations in 1998. *Yuriy Kirsanov*

Aerofax
ILYUSHIN IL-18/20/22
A Versatile Turboprop Transport

Yefim Gordon and Dmitriy Komissarov

The IL-18 four-turboprop airliner first flew in 1957 and was supplied to many 'friendly nations' in Eastern Europe, Asia, Africa, Middle East and the Caribbean. Its uses included passenger and cargo, VIP transportation, support of Antarctic research stations, electronic espionage and various research programmes. All versions are described, as are many test and development aircraft, the IL-20M ELINT, IL-20RT space tracker, IL-22 airborne command post, IL-24N for ice reconnaissance and IL-38 ASW aircraft.

Softback, 280 x 215 mm, 160 pages
184 b/w, 67 colour photos, 16pp dwgs
1 85780 157 1 **£19.99**

Aerofax
TUPOLEV Tu-134
The USSR's Short-Range Jet Airliner

Dmitriy Komissarov

The Tu-134 has seen passenger service for over 35 years in 42 countries. Its multifarious other activities include VIP transportation, support of Air Force, Army and Navy headquarters and research and test work. The type has helped train thousands of military pilots and navigators for the Soviet Air Forces' tactical and long-range bomber forces.

Compiled from first-hand Russian sources, the book gives a full account of the Tu-134 and the type's design, test and operational history.

Sbk, 280 x 215 mm, 184pp, 204 col, 95 b/w photos, 5pp of drawings
1 85780 159 8 **£19.99**

Aerofax
ILYUSHIN IL-76
Russia's Versatile Jet Freighter

Yefim Gordon and Dmitriy Komissarov

The Soviet Union's answer to the Lockheed Starlifter first flew in 1971 and has become familiar both in its intended military guise and as a commercial freighter. It has also been developed as the IL-78 for aerial refuelling, and in AEW and other versions.

There is not only a full development history and technical description, but extensive tables detailing each aircraft built, with c/n, serial and so on, and detailed notes on every operator, both civil and military, and their fleets.

Softback, 280 x 215 mm, 160 pages
c250 b/w and colour photos, drawings
1 85780 106 7 **£19.95**

AIRLINES WORLDWIDE
Over 360 Airlines Described and Illustrated in Colour (4th edition)

B I Hengi

Airlines Worldwide, first published in 1994, has established itself as a trusted and sought-after reference work. It aims to give an overview and illustrate the world's leading or more interesting airlines, including smaller national operators, with their history, routes, aircraft fleet and operations.

This latest edition is more than ever revised and updated, notably in the light of the turbulent events and rapid changes in the airline industry over the past couple of years.

Softback, 240 x 170 mm, 384 pages
c360 full colour photographs
1 85780 155 5 **£18.99**

Red Star Volume 12
ANTONOV'S TURBOPROP TWINS – An-24/26/30/32

Yefim Gordon

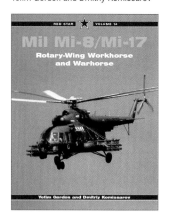

The twin-turboprop An-24 was designed in the late 1950s and was produced by three Soviet aircraft factories; many remain in operation.

The An-24 airliner evolved first into the 'quick fix' An-24T and then into the An-26. This paved the way for the 'hot and high' An-32 and the 'big head' An-30, the latter for aerial photography.

This book lists all known operators of Antonov's twin-turboprop family around the world.

Softback, 280 x 215 mm, 128 pages
175 b/w and 28 colour photographs, plus line drawings
1 85780 153 9 **£18.99**

Red Star Volume 14
MIL Mi-8/Mi-17
Rotary-Wing Workhorse and Warhorse

Yefim Gordon and Dmitriy Komissarov

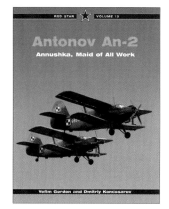

Since 1961, when it first took to the air, the basic design of the Mi-8 has evolved. Every known version, both civil and military, is covered, including electronic warfare, minelaying and minesweeping and SAR. It also served as a basis for the Mi-14 amphibious ASW helicopter.

Over the years the Mi-8 family have become veritable aerial workhorses, participating in countless wars of varying scale. The type is probably best known for its service in the Afghan War.

Softback, 280 x 215 mm, 128 pages
179 b/w and 32 colour photographs, plus line drawings
1 85780 161 X **£18.99**

Red Star Volume 15
ANTONOV AN-2
Annushka, Maid of All Work

Yefim Gordon and Dmitriy Komissarov

Initially derided as 'obsolete at the moment of birth' due to its biplane layout, this aircraft has put the sceptics to shame. It may lack the glamour of the fast jets, but it has proved itself time and time again as an indispensable and long-serving workhorse. The An-2, which first flew in 1947, has been operated by more than 40 nations.

The An-2 is the only biplane transport which remained in service long enough to pass into the 21st century!

Softback, 280 x 215 mm, 128 pages
200 b/w and 28 colour photographs, plus line drawings.
1 85780 162 8 **£18.99**